This Is My Boy

By
Miguel Crespo

TEACH Services, Inc.
PUBLISHING
www.TEACHServices.com • (800) 367-1844

Copyright © 2004 TEACH Services, Inc.
ISBN-13: 978-1-5725-8286-6 (Paperback)
Library of Congress Control Number: 2004108039

TEACH Services, Inc.
P U B L I S H I N G
www.TEACHServices.com • (800) 367-1844

Contents

Contents

Introduction

I believe that in every Christian's experience there has to come a time when he or she decides whether or not he or she truly believes in God. What I mean is that as Christians we believe that there's a God who cares about us. However, in reality many Christians only believe in God when things are going well. When times get hard one of the first things we do is question His existence. We question whether or not He listens to our prayers. We allow ourselves to wonder if we've been wasting our time going to church all these years. *"If God can't help me when I'm in trouble, then what good is He?"* is the question that runs through the mind. The Bible is full of stories of servants of the Lord who endured great loss in His service, but that somehow doesn't seem to connect with most of us, especially those of us living in North America. In North America the popular thinking is that if something bad is happening to you then it's because you are not being faithful to God. But in nearly every other part of the world suffering is accepted as an essential part of being a Christian. If you are <u>not</u> suffering in some way then you are not living the way you should be. When we experience trials the temptation for us (living in North America) is to look to ourselves for the solution; to blame God for His lack of involvement in our lives. We sever our relationship with God because He "wasn't there for us." How dare God do such a thing like this? To me!! —How tragic! What really needs to occur in a Christian's life during a time of crisis is exactly the reverse. And that is to run to God and spend a lot of time on our knees; praying and pleading for strength, and faith to overcome.

There is a saying in the military, "The more you sweat during peace time, the less you bleed during wartime". This means that if you take the time to prepare yourself for the conflict during the times of peace, when the time of conflict comes you'll be better prepared to survive it. Take it from me, when a crisis hits your life, that's not the time to question your core beliefs. When your world seems like it's crashing down around you, that's not the time to utter these little mealy mouth, wimpy, half believing prayers to heaven.

In this book I would like to share an experience that my family and I went through. It was a difficult time for us. It was a time when I had my faith tested, a time when I had to confront all those questions that come up when your world seems turned upside down. *Does God really care about me? How much attention does He really pay to what's going on in my life? Does prayer really accomplish anything? Am I willing to suffer loss and still believe in and trust Him?* I learned a lot about myself in that year and a half. I'd like to say that throughout the whole ordeal I was a perfect example of what a Christian should be, but there were times…sometimes it seems that God is so far away! —I want you to know that even though it may feel that way you can be sure that the difficult times in our lives are when God is the closest…comforting, protecting, making a way for us to get through. Praise the Lord!!!

I will admit to you beforehand that I am a child at heart. My wife prefers the word 'immature', or 'weird', but I prefer to say I'm a child at heart. Even when I'm serious I seem to interject humor into a situation. I guess that's how I deal with stress. You will see that that's how I write. I also do not think in a straight line. I sometimes go off into tangents. Forgive me, I am trying to write my experiences as they happened, the stray thoughts entered here and there are part of that experience.

I hope that as you read this story you will be encouraged to trust in the Lord more fully. I expect that you probably will at points understand what I was going through because you have possibly experienced something similar. At other times you may not understand at all. —But when the trials come to you, you will. And when the trials come to you I pray that you will remember this story and use it to stand firm and trust in the only living God, though the heavens fall.

The Breaking Point

We were singing in the chapel… *"Why is there a giant moose head in the chapel?"* I thought to myself. *"The head of a large dead animal seems a little out of place in a place of worship…."* The words *"Thou shalt not kill"* keep resounding in my head. *"Somebody should talk to the camp director… The chapel does look nice though, it has a rustic, country look."* You could see the tongue and groove wood paneling was aged and could use a coat of polyurethane, but that just gave the building character. The beams overhead were actually logs that had been cut down and shaped to fit above the frame. *"They didn't even shave the bark off… Cool!"*

As the group began to sing a chorus I suddenly heard a voice in my head say, *"If you love Me, you have to let Nathaniel go! Do you love Me?"* Finally, I lost it, I knew then that I was going to lose my son! I picked up my sleeping, 14 month-old baby boy and just ran out of that room, tears streaming down my face. It was as if the levee had broken; I couldn't stop the tears, I was out of control. That same voice kept echoing in my head, *"Do you love Me? You have to let him go!"*

This was the breaking point for me. I had put my trust in God and refused to let any negative thoughts into my head. I would not consider even for a moment that my son might be taken from me. But this… God had spoken to me! I had to decide; do I trust God completely or not? If God allows my son to be taken from me, will I still serve Him? Worship Him? Love Him? If I loved God, I had to let Nathaniel go…. Did I love Him?

The Beginning

In order to understand what the preceding section was all about, it's necessary to start at the beginning, the very beginning. It was 1996. I don't remember what part of the year it was, but my wife could tell you. She's the detail person. For example, she could tell you when our children were born; the year, the day, the hour. I just know they were born. When our second son, Jacob, was born we decided that his middle name was going to be Matthew. Well, I didn't find out until he was two years old that Matthew was spelled with two T's, not one. I had a wanted poster made up with the pictures of both of our sons, Joshua, and Jacob. My wife saw how I spelled Jacob's middle name and quickly corrected me. She was mad too! —I don't worry about the details as much as she does. Now, if you want details on important things, like sports, then I'm your guy.

Anyway, I remember having a conversation with my wife one evening when she laid what I thought was a bombshell on me. "I want to adopt a baby!"… Apparently she had done her homework also. "Our County has a foster parent class that certifies you and allows you to adopt children who need homes in the foster care system."

"What! Are you crazy?" I believe is how I started my part of the conversation. As we discussed the pros and cons of adoption my wife pointed out that we should, as Christians, seek to help others and share our blessings with those less fortunate, and I pointed out all the dangers and inconveniences involved in taking in other people's children. I remember at one point asking, "Why do you want more children? I don't like the ones I got right now!" And again she reminded me of how as Christians we should do more than just talk; we should do things for our fellow man… I don't remember the totality of how our conversation went, details remember, but I do remember putting my foot down and saying, "NO! Absolutely not!"

Now I thought that was the end of it. After all, I am the head of the house; I am in charge! Well, since that time I have learned a very important lesson. And that is that if the husband is the head of the house, then the wife is the neck. And the neck can make the head do anything it wants to....

I came home from work the next day and my wife didn't say much to me. She wasn't angry; she just wasn't talking much. When I asked her what we were having for supper, she just looked at me with those beautifully cold blue eyes, and with a very unconcerned look said, "I already fed the boys."

"Well, what about me?" I asked.

"You can have cereal if you want..."

"You're mad at me, aren't you?"

"Now why would I be mad at you? Just because you cut me off and won't even consider adoption?... That's fine..."

And so, it began...for three days straight I would have to eat either cereal, or make something myself (I don't cook very well). And during those three days she probably said four words to me; "Good morning", and "Good night."

Finally at the end of the three days, emaciated and defeated, I came up to her and, with my tail between my legs, said, "You—you know – uh—I—I'm thinking that we should give this foster parenting thing a try. Yeah, I—I—I think it's a good idea."...and that is how this whole adventure began....

Looking back, I've come to realize that there are few things that have done more for my spiritual growth than becoming a foster parent. In order to become foster parents, we had to attend some classes that taught us how to deal with children who have been traumatized, either by abuse, or by the very fact that they've been taken from their homes to another family. It's tough for those little people. It's sad how the young have to suffer because of the indifference or ignorance of their parents.

I have to admit that at the beginning I didn't want to go to the foster parents' class. I was more interested in building my power tool collection (I had four or five at the time), than in taking on more responsibilities. But I want to share with you that as I kept going to those classes I realized that there is a tremendous need out there. And I wish that Christians were more active in this arena. I remember one time in our training class… It wasn't a very large room. There were six or seven couples there; Bonnie couldn't make it so I was alone that night. We were all sitting around a large conference table. The table was so large that we could barely fit the chairs between the edges of the table and the four walls. Our instructor, a Child Protective Services social worker, was leading out. One of the subjects we touched on was the importance of religion in our life. As the different couples in that small, musty room began to respond to her questions I realized that most of these families did not claim any particular religion. Some may not even have believed in God at all. They were just interested in helping to protect children, and in offering themselves and their homes to these children that they had no relation to. As I sat there and let that realization sink into me, I cannot describe the depth of my shame…. Here I am, a Seventh-day Adventist Christian, claiming to love Christ, claiming to believe that we are here to help those around us, but not being willing to put myself out for those less fortunate. *"What a hypocrite!"* I thought. Up until that time I had thought I was a good Christian. I went to church, paid my tithe; any time they needed someone to help out up front, I would never say no. I'm a friendly person; I don't swear—I even preach a sermon in church now and then. But is that what being a Christian is all about? I thought so…. However, I've learned that the Bible gives us a different answer. James 1:27 states "Pure religion and undefiled before God and the Father is this, *to visit the fatherless and widows in their affliction*, and to keep himself unspotted from the world."

I was too busy with **my** wants, **my** desires, to worry about taking care of those who have real needs. What a joke! Romans

2:13 plainly states, "For not the hearers of the law are just before God, but the *doers* of the law shall be justified." In modern language we might say, "You can't just talk the talk, you gotta walk the walk." A person that does not put into practice what he, or she is preaching is nothing but a hypocrite! And that is what I saw myself as. Needless to say, I decided that night that foster parenting really was the right thing to do.

It was three years later that we adopted a little girl, Hannah. At that point I thought that we were done. I thought our family was complete. We had three children, Joshua, Jacob, and Hannah, and any more would be irresponsible and foolish.

Just when life started getting back to normal...

Let us fast-forward five years, to 2001. My wife and I had been foster parents the whole time. By this time we had had seven or eight children in our home for varying lengths of time. We didn't adopt any; these were just short-term placements. After we adopted Hannah we had planned to stop being foster parents, but we just couldn't walk away from the foster care program. The fact is that there are always more children in need of homes than there are homes to take them in. So we became what they call "respite providers." We took in foster children when their 'real' foster parents needed a break or when children needed short term care; sometimes a weekend, sometimes a few months… I grew quite attached to some of the kids we had stay with us. I frequently gave them nicknames based on their characteristics. Sometimes the names weren't very flattering, but they were always given in love! One was named Jill. I named her "Jill the Pill", and she was too. I remember Paige; she was a chunky, blond, almost white haired eight-month old. One day I told my wife that she was too big to be called just 'Paige' so I dubbed her, "Chapter." I remember Jonathan. I changed his name to "Penguin boy" because he waddled around the house. We had one boy named Eric. He reminded me of one of the munchkins from the movie "The Wizard of Oz". He had a big blond curl that stuck up on the front of his head, almost like the tail of the soft-serve ice cream when they serve it in a cone. I tried to teach him to swing his arm and sing, "We're from the lollipop guild, the lollipop guild…" While I grew attached to them, I did not have, nor did I want the opportunity to adopt any more children.

On March 20, 2001 (my wife provided all the dates used in this book), we received a phone call that a little baby had been born and had come into care, and they wanted us to take him right from the hospital. At the time the call came in we were in town, about one mile away from the hospital, at the mall. Because we didn't get the message, they had to call someone else to take in this, as-yet-anonymous child. When my wife found out that we had missed this opportunity, she was heartbroken; she loves babies. It didn't bother me. I love playing with babies—don't get me wrong—but they require a lot of attention. And with the addition of Hannah, I was already demoted one more level. I was already fighting for my wife's affections; one more makes it that much more difficult. I quickly forgot about it. I just figured it was God's will that that baby wasn't meant to be in our home. Bonnie, however, did not forget…. *Was it God's will for us to take in this baby? Didn't God know where we were going to be? If it was meant to be wouldn't Social Services have called when we were home? Were we not supposed to be at the mall that day?*

At the end of April, Bonnie was called and asked if we would provide respite care for a baby whose foster parents were going on vacation. My wife, as usual said yes, and then called me to ask me if I thought we should do it or not. "This is the same baby they called us on last month!" she said. "His name is Nathaniel…"

Nathaniel

Well, Nathaniel came to visit us for a couple of days. He was just over a month old. He was such a small thing! He was as pale as a sheet and had a full head of jet-black hair. His eyes were brown, but they were so dark they looked as if you were staring into two shiny orbs of volcanic glass. His head was constantly turned to one side. It almost looked as if his head was on backwards. The doctor said that it was because of how he had been positioned in the womb. He was always in that position. Poor boy! He also had a serious skin problem. He had eczema, and it was really bad. His skin looked as though he had rough little scales on him. This was all over his body.

During the respite, Bonnie took care of him. I helped from time to time, but I didn't really get involved. I don't recall anything special about that visit. To me Nathaniel was just like any of the other children that we had boarded.

In late June we received another call. Nathaniel's foster parents were going away again; they needed respite and requested Bonnie and me to take care of him. This time it would be for a whole week. As usual, Bonnie said yes and later informed me that we were going to be taking care of him. "I am not changing diapers!" I said. Because he had been with us for such a short time before I hadn't had to do diaper duty, but I had a feeling that sometime in that week I would have to do it. And sure enough, I did.

I can't explain to you what happened that week. I never saw it coming. I thought that my family was complete, that my life was perfect. I had (have) a great wife, great kids. God had blessed me with a job that allowed my wife to stay home and care for the children. The last thing I wanted was to add another child to our family. But apparently God had other plans….

From the time that I gave my heart to the Lord, I believed that He had a plan for my life. I believe that He has a plan for everyone's life. God has a place for all of us in the drama that is playing out on this earth. I believe that there are souls we are given the responsibility to reach. We each have a post to fill in the great battle against sin. And those plans are revealed to us on a 'need-to-know' basis. Sometimes the path before us is clear, other times it's not. Sometimes God throws us a curve ball. In my case, God threw me a 105 mph fast-ball right down the middle. And it caught me totally by surprise! I'll share this much. What God had planned for me was not what I had planned for myself.

It happened sometime during that week. I had just finished feeding Nathaniel when I got a whiff of that telltale odor that told me that it was that time again… "Oh man! —Bonnie? —**Bonnie!?!** —**Oh man!!!** (After a long exhale) Let's go Nathaniel, it's time for a diaper change." I took him into our bedroom and laid him on the bed. Something happened there, and I still can't explain it. As I was changing Nathaniel's diaper he just lay there and looked up at me. It was one of those rare times when he actually straightened out his neck and was able to look straight ahead. I remember looking into those deep, dark brown eyes of his…they were so bright! As I was looking at him I heard a voice in my head say, *"This is your son!"* I heard it as clear as a bell! For a brief moment his eyes met my eyes, I felt as if I had found a long lost son, *"This is my son!"* I said to myself… For some reason I wanted to cry, I was excited! *"What just happened?"* I thought to myself… I didn't understand. Now, I am not someone given to emotion. In fact, I can be quite hard hearted, especially when compared with my wife. While Bonnie cared very much for Nathaniel she had not said anything to me in regard to taking him in if he was freed for adoption. I am also not one to go around telling people that God **speaks** to me. I thought that God only spoke to people like Moses, or the prophets. I know myself; I am not a Moses, and I most certainly do not have it together enough to be a mouthpiece for God. But I can't explain it any other way. I heard someone speak to me that day. It had to be God because the other alternative would be too horrible to contemplate.

I immediately found Bonnie (it's funny how I couldn't find her when his diaper needed changing but after I was done, there she was) and said to her, "I don't know what Nathaniel's future is going to be, but if he is freed for adoption he's coming to live with us! Understand?"

My wife looked at me half surprised, half puzzled. "You make it sound like I don't want him to stay. That's fine! But Michelle [Nathaniel's foster mom] said that he isn't free for adoption. He's going back to his family."

"I don't care!" I don't know why I was yelling at Bonnie. "I'm just tellin' you that this is my boy! And if he is gonna be adopted, he's gonna be adopted into this family!"

Bonnie got this big grin on her face. She loved Nathaniel too! I don't remember much about the rest of that week except that it went by much too fast, and my heart ached when it was time for Nathaniel to go back to his foster home. That little boy had wormed his way into my heart. I didn't know what was going to happen in the future, but I knew one thing: our family was not complete without Nathaniel! I prayed that the Lord would watch over him, and, if he was going to be adopted, that He would give us the opportunity to be his mom and dad.

Because Nathaniel did not come to our house directly from the hospital in March, my wife and I both believed, at the time, that it was God's will for Nathaniel to be somewhere else. I strongly believe that we should never run ahead of the Lord. If it's God's will for a certain thing to take place, the Lord will see to it. So I confess that I was conflicted between my conviction that Nathaniel should be here, and my belief that, if he was meant to be here he would have come to our home directly from the hospital. This issue hung like a cloud over Bonnie and me throughout the whole ordeal that this book is concerned with.

About a week after Nathaniel left, Bonnie received a phone call from Nathaniel's foster mom. She told Bonnie that the judge had changed Nathaniel's goal from reunification with his mother to adoption. Bonnie told me later that she hoped she had done the right thing. For you see, when she finished speaking with Michelle, she immediately called Social Services and told the Case Worker that we wanted to be considered as a possible placement for Nathaniel. She loved Nathaniel, but she didn't want to run ahead of God. (If God wanted him to be with us, wouldn't He impress those in charge of Nathaniel's case to call us?) But she also knew that if she didn't call and I found out, I'd probably have a coronary attack. —I believe that God's plans take into account the actions of men and women who are trying to do what is best. Nathaniel came back to our home near the end of July, and we committed ourselves to adopting him when the time came.

Nathaniel's situation was a little bit different in that they had not finished looking at other placement options for him. If a child cannot be returned to a parent for any reason, Social Services is required to determine whether there are any other family members who can take him in. And so when the Case Worker for Nathaniel met with Bonnie and me she informed us that we needed to understand that we were taking him in for an adoption, but that there was a possibility that he might go to a family member. I remember the case worker saying, "This is difficult. You have to raise him as your own, but he may be taken away. You may find if you get too close that it will tear you apart if, and when he has to go."

"It's too late!" I told her. "If Nathaniel left right now, I would be heartbroken!"

The next four months were some of the happiest in my life. I found myself longing to be home when I was at work, and I couldn't wait to get home and see all of my children, all four of them.

The Phone call

Nathaniel was officially placed in our home on July 27th. Actually, he came back home on the 20th, but the paperwork was not filled out until the 27th. This becomes very important later on. Anyway, life at the Crespo home began to fall into a normal routine. The kids were crazy about the new baby. I would come home from work and the kids and I would spend the next two or three hours on the floor playing, wrestling, or giving horsie rides to "Godzilla". That was the name I had given Nathaniel. Whenever he got mad or wanted a toy back that someone had taken away he would let out a yell that reminded me of the old Godzilla movies. We really did become one big happy family.

The next four months were as exciting as they were fleeting. I had decided to return to college beginning in January, and was making preparations for that. We had also planned on visiting my mother for Thanksgiving and were making plans for the six-hour trip to her house. Most of the preparations for that trip were mental. Four kids, one car, six hours…it had been awhile since we had gone on a trip like that and I was dreading the 125 "are we there yets?", and the 230 "I have to go to the bathroom's." We were also a little anxious because we had heard very little about Nathaniel's situation. Social Services' was still researching placement options for him.

So Thanksgiving came and went. We had a great time at my mother's house…. I don't think she totally agreed with the idea of taking on another child…or maybe she just didn't understand the reason for taking him in. I hadn't told anyone except Bonnie about the revelation I had when I was changing Nathaniel.

I spent a lot of time in prayer and praise during those four months. I was so happy at how everything was working out that I found myself constantly praising the Lord. I had a hard time formulating proper prayers because I just wanted to thank Him for all the wonderful blessings He had bestowed, especially on one as undeserving as me. I felt that it wasn't enough just to say 'thank you', I felt I had to do something to show Him just how thankful I was. At one point I contemplated writing "Thank you Lord" one million times, just to show God how I appreciated what he had done for me. (I know, childish right?) I came to the conclusion that this would be silly and unnecessary because He knew how I felt. —I remember thinking that life just couldn't get any better than this! —It's easy to praise the Lord when things are going your way!

On November 27th, Bonnie received the phone call that we had hoped would never come. It was from the Social Worker, who told her that they had found relatives for Nathaniel (an aunt and uncle) who were willing to take him in. They lived down in Tennessee. Bonnie's heart sank down to her feet! The Case Worker said that she would be mailing the paperwork to these people so that they could file for custody. Bonnie later described the Case Worker as matter of fact about it when she called…she didn't even express that she was sorry for what we were about to go through!

On that day I had traveled three hours away to do a service call. And it was there that I received the frantic phone call from my wife. An aunt and uncle had expressed interest in Nathaniel. Nathaniel was going to leave! When Bonnie called me I was in the middle of an install of a printer on a customer's computer network. I had to install it and show them how to use it. I couldn't afford to break down and get all emotional at this point. I had a job to do. I might have been in a state of shock also. I confess that as I robotically went through the motions of doing my job I had many thoughts run through my head. *"Why God? How could you have allowed this to happen? Why is it that Bonnie always calls me with bad news when I'm miles away and can't be there for her? Please don't let my son go…"* I couldn't wait to get done with this install so that I could go home. I remember that as I was driving back I rehearsed the scene that took place in my bedroom when I had heard God's voice. *"I didn't imagine that! God spoke to me! Nathaniel **is** my son! —But Bonnie said that the Social Worker told her Nathaniel would be leaving...?"* Social Services said one thing, but God, I thought, said another. Who was I going to believe...? I decided to believe God. *"This is going to make a great sermon!"*, I thought to myself. God would come through and save the day and I would use this experience to encourage others.... I chose to practice what I had been preaching. I would like to say that I leaned totally on my faith in God, but I didn't. I was hoping that the paperwork would get lost in the mail, or that Nathaniel's relatives would change their mind. Just because they expressed an interest in Nathaniel didn't mean that he was definitely leaving. I decided to put my faith in God and wait and see how things developed. In other words, I wasn't going to flip out until I knew for sure my son was leaving.

The Dedication

On November 29th, we had our pastor come to our home and dedicate Nathaniel. We had planned to do this about a month before. However, it now seemed more important than ever to dedicate him because of the possibility that he was leaving. I'm not sure how other denominations do it but in the Adventist church a minister will 'dedicate' a baby instead of baptizing him or her. We do this because we feel that baptism is an act of the will of the person being baptized, not the will of the parents. In our church we dedicate our children (babies) to the Lord's service, but in reality what we are doing is stating that the parents are making a commitment before God that they will endeavor to raise the child in the nurture of the Lord and His Scriptures.

When Pastor T. came to our house I wanted him to dedicate Nathaniel to the Lord. I wanted Nathaniel to be placed in the Lord's care, wherever he would go. I thought that dedication meant that he was set apart as one of God's chosen. And that meant that wherever he went, God would watch over him and make sure that he was protected. Pastor T. quickly informed me that dedication was done more for the parents than for the child. He said, "You are making a declaration to the Lord that you will raise him in accordance with the teachings in the Scriptures. You are the ones really being dedicated here, to teach Nathaniel about God." —Man, was I bummed out! I had too much respect for him to tell him I didn't want him to dedicate me! I wanted him to somehow ask for a special blessing on this boy. I wanted Nathaniel to be given his very own company of angels, guardians that would protect him and look out for him throughout the rest of his life. —I didn't understand what dedication was all about, but I never told the pastor about my expectations. We agreed to dedicate ourselves to raising Nathaniel as a Christian. But in the

back of my mind I wondered how long we would have him to do that.

The reason we had Nathaniel dedicated at home instead of at church was that he was legally not our son. We didn't want it to get back to Social Services that we had done this. They wouldn't have understood it. We felt that his dedication was important though, so we had a private dedication at home. Looking back it is a great memory: Bonnie and I standing in our living room in front of the preacher with eight-month old Nathaniel in our arms and our three children standing as our witnesses behind us. Behind all of us, the picture window looking out over our backyard, with the pine and maple trees gently waving in the cool autumn breeze, silent witnesses to the heartache and joy that we were going to experience in the next year. —It kind of looked like a shotgun wedding!

How do I deal with this?

I don't know if I can properly explain what we were feeling about this time.... Imagine finding out that your child has a terminal disease...you don't know how much time you have but you know that it's less than you would want. Even though I believed that God wanted Nathaniel to be a part of our family, I wasn't 100% convinced. Why didn't he come to our home right from the hospital? Why did we have to call Social Services to tell them we wanted him? Were we really in the Lord's will with this? Bonnie and I spent many evenings going over these questions, trying to find answers to them. Just when we thought we had come to grips with certain issues, we had to face them all over again.

One concern I had was for Nathaniel's future. What if the family he went to weren't Christians? If he's taken from our home he would be lost to us, but he might also be lost eternally! That thought drove me crazy! I wanted to scream at times. I thought about my faith...did I still trust in God? What had seemed to be a blessing from God now seemed like a curse! I no longer praised the Lord. My prayers were more like pitiful pleas for Him to do something, anything for my situation. Sometimes I would find myself out on my lawn at night, looking up at the stars, standing among the silent witnesses. Not knowing what to say, afraid I'd start cussing God out for abandoning me to the wolves, so to speak. I was desperate! My whole world seemed to be in disorder. When I felt almost ready to explode, I would remember that there is only one Person that can bring order to my disorderly life. It would be foolish to turn away from the only One that can help me. So in my mental struggle the only word I could mutter out would be, "Please!!!!" I am ashamed to admit that there were many times when I hit this wall where I found

myself thinking, *"Why don't you just curse God and forget Him!"* I came perilously close to walking away from my faith! I've never told anyone that.

Although the Case Worker sent the paperwork to the Johnsons she had not heard from them for that whole month so we spent the month of December in a sort of limbo. I believed that God had answered my prayer and diverted the paperwork from Tennessee to Alaska, or someplace else. So since we hadn't received any news, we decided that we were going to make whatever time we had with Nathaniel enjoyable and went ahead with our plans for Christmas, and I still planned on going to school in January.

I would like to share a little about the relationship that we had with Nathaniel at this time. It should go without stating that Bonnie and I loved Nathaniel. He was as much a part of our family as the other children. But it's true that loving a child completely is not easy to do when you know that the child is going to be taken away. There is a part of you that is afraid to love completely because of the fear of the pain that will have to be dealt with after all is said and done. Nathaniel was seven or eight months old at the time. I remember asking myself how I should relate to this boy. —Emotions are a funny thing —emotional pain in some ways is worse to experience than physical pain, and emotional scars take longer to heal than the physical ones. —I made up my mind that I would not entertain any negative thoughts. I decided to have faith and trust that my God would work things out. I really didn't have any other option in dealing with this because every time my mind went down that road I would feel a pain that I can only describe as an anvil sitting on my chest. I had trouble breathing...my chest would feel tight. *"Is this a heart attack?"* I felt as if the whole world was crashing in on my head. *"Am I losing my mind?"* I could feel my head begin to pound...my mind began to race... I felt that my heart was being literally crushed! So I decided for that reason not to allow my mind to entertain negative thoughts. I mentally set up a barrier that would block any attempts by my mind to go down that path. I was afraid that it might literally kill me!

But then how should I relate to Nathaniel? The closer I got to him, the harder it was to maintain that barrier against negative thoughts. Every time I kissed him, every time I smelled him, every time that he looked at me and held his arms out to me, my heart would melt, and inevitably the waves of doubt and despair would beat against that barrier: huge, crushing waves of uncertainty and a fearful looking forward into a future without my son!

There was an easier way to deal with this. I could just not get too close to him. I could just stop loving him and treat him like any other foster child that we've had in our home. This would be so much easier. No attachment, no pain…no shattered pieces to pick up after he left. But what about Nathaniel? A child needs love to develop properly. At that age a baby needs to bond with his parents. One thing that many foster children suffer from is the inability to form proper attachments. This comes from the lack of bonding when they are very young. If I keep Nathaniel at arms' length until he leaves…the damage done to his psyche may have long lasting effects. He might never be able to bond with anyone! Bonnie and I talked about this at length. We decided that it would be wrong to keep Nathaniel at an emotional arms' length. That would be selfish; it just wouldn't be fair to him. Although the loss of Nathaniel would be devastating to us, we would get over it a lot easier than he would because we're adults. Besides, our love for him demanded that we expose ourselves to this pain. At this point I couldn't stop loving him if I tried. This was another burden I carried throughout this time. I knew that loving Nathaniel came at a cost. A cost that I wasn't sure I could pay, and live through. But what choice did I have?

When I think of this I can't help but think of Jesus Christ. He had a choice…. He chose to expose Himself to the pain and humiliation of the cross because His love for mankind (for you and for me) was greater than His love for Himself. He could have stayed away, and let sin run its course and destroy us, but His love compelled Him to fight for us. And I think of the Father, who allowed Christ to be beaten, whipped, and ridiculed, to save a rebellious race. What do you think hurts more, to suffer affliction yourself or to watch your child suffer? I gained a little better insight into what Jesus and the Father went through because of this experience. God loves us more than He loves His very life. Jesus paid a heavy price because of His love for the human race. O love that wilt not let me go!

Our little time of trouble

This is the part that I believe is the most challenging. I want to relate the events that took place, but those events are meaningless if they are not tied to the feelings that I experienced throughout them.

I had made up my mind to put my trust in the Lord. I believed that He would ultimately work things out. What I really meant was that I believed that my son would continue to be a part of my family. Even though I told my wife that I trusted that the Lord would do what was in Nathaniel's best interests, I expected Nathaniel would stay. That was in his best interests. I refused to even think about Nate's going away. Every time doubt crept into my mind and I began to think, *"What if...,"* I would quickly shake my head and think about something else. I don't know if that's called faith or if it's more like living in denial, but that's what I did from the months of December to June. I remember one weekend when Bonnie planned on going into town and taking the kids' pictures. She asked me if she should let Nathaniel be in the pictures with the rest of the kids (since he might leave, and then any photos lying around the house would destroy us every time we looked at them). I told her that it was a sign of a lack of faith if we didn't include him in our family photos. I was angry that she would even ask such a thing. I wanted to show God that I trusted in Him. The Bible states that we are a spectacle to men and to angels. I believe that through this ordeal God was watching us, to see if we really trusted Him. The inclusion of Nathaniel in our family photos that year was a sign to God that we were walking by faith, not sight.

For the entire month of December we had not heard anything about the custody procedure. Bonnie would call the Case Worker now and then to find out what was going on, but it was always the

Endless Court Appearances

The first court date was scheduled for February 11. Even though we had been foster parents for several years, we had never been present at any of the court hearings that had to do with the children in our care. I thought that the judge would make his ruling that day. I couldn't have been more wrong. The wheels of the court system move forward, but they do so ever so slowly! First they have to rule that Nathaniel's biological parents cannot take custody of him. Then they have to decide where they are going to place him. If a family member is found, that family member has to have a background check and a home study completed to determine whether or not he or she can actually provide for him. This process requires a lot of paperwork and many hearings before a judge. What I thought to be a sprint turned out to be a marathon and I was bothered by this; Nathaniel was going to stay with us for quite awhile now. This meant it would be harder for all of us. —This was just one more burden that I had to carry.—If Nathaniel was going to leave, I wanted him to go as soon as possible to minimize the pain that all of us were going to feel. But now he was going to be that much more bonded with us, and we would be that much more bonded with him.

The first time that I went before Judge William Lawless I didn't know what to expect. It was a brand new experience for me, and I don't mind telling you that I was nervous. I thought my son was leaving, and I was afraid that it would happen and I wouldn't be able to even address the judge. When I found out what the Judge's name was, I kind of chuckled that there would be a judge with the name of Lawless! (By the way, his father was the County Sheriff. Imagine, a lawman with the last name of Lawless!)

Bonnie and I had done some homework before this hearing. According to the law, foster parents cannot legally interfere in a court proceeding relating to a child in their home unless that child has been in their home for twelve consecutive months. Nathaniel had been in our home for about six months. While we could not interfere, we did have the right to be present at any proceeding that related to a child in our care. So I told Bonnie to let the Case Worker know that I would be there. I don't know how the Case Worker felt about that and I really didn't care. She knew how we felt about Nathaniel. I decided I was going to see this thing through. My hope was that if the judge or one of the lawyers saw how important this was to us, then maybe they might help us. This was completely new for me. I had no idea what to expect.

When I went to family court for the first time, I was surprised to see just how many people were there. *"Holy Moly! All these people are here for court? These people (Social Services) never get a break!"* I thought. I looked for Judge Lawless' court-room…when I walked in, I was surprised at how small it was. The room is probably forty feet by forty feet. As you walk in, you see to the right two slightly curved tables facing the judge's bench, which is further to the right. On the left side is the back wall of the courtroom, which is lined with chairs. Between the curved tables and the judge's bench, to their left, is another table. I soon found out what each of these tables was for. The two curved tables were for the plaintiffs, defendants, and their lawyers. The table to the left of these was for the Law Guardian. Each child in foster care is given a Law Guardian. His job is to objectively look at the facts surrounding the child's case and give the judge his recommendation as to what would be in the child's best interest.

It was at this hearing that I met Nathaniel's biological mother. During the different hearings I got to meet both of Nathaniel's biological parents. I met each of them once. The only fact I would like to share is that they were not fit to take care of him. Everyone agreed with that. I saw them once, and in the next six months I never saw them again. They never showed up at any of the court dates.

At that hearing nothing was really decided; the biological mother wanted to have an attorney represent her, so the judge postponed the hearing until she got legal counsel. As I said before, the bio-mom never showed up before the court again. The attorney representing her didn't have any explanation for her absence. I took notes of every hearing that I went to. I wanted to be able to document what happened because – well, I'm not exactly sure why. I know that I didn't want to forget this experience. I was also hoping I could keep a record so that I could share it with Nathaniel when he got older and began to ask questions. I mentally sized up every person that was present at the hearing.

The first, obviously, was Judge Lawless. He seemed rather young to me to be a judge; somewhere in his early to mid-forties. One look at him told you that he took his job very seriously. He didn't hesitate to rip into the Social Services attorneys if he felt they weren't doing something right. Which seemed kind of strange to me because I would have thought them to be on the same side. I came to understand that Judge Lawless was partial to no one, except the law. (Which I guess you have to be in that position.)

The attorney who represented Social Services was Jack Day. He was a rather friendly person. When I first met him I wasn't sure how he would act towards me because I really had no business being there. However, he gave me a firm handshake and greeted me warmly! I liked him in spite of the fact that I hated him for trying to remove my son from my home.

The Case Worker for Nathaniel was Angela Dow. I didn't like her at first! Every time that Bonnie would speak with her she would be very matter of fact about Nathaniel's leaving. She never showed any emotion. At first I thought it was because she didn't like us. Every time Bonnie related a conversation she had with this woman, I would get upset because we seemingly got nowhere with her. You would think that after all these years of taking in kids she would have done something for us. Or at least tried to empathize with us. I really didn't like her! However, as time went on I began to understand her a little bit better. I can say now that she is a great lady! Unfortunately, her job is one that demands a certain amount of emotional detachment; otherwise she might end up in the loony bin. I don't envy her position.

The Law Guardian for Nathaniel was David Packer. He was a tall, thin man. His job was to look out for Nathaniel. I felt that he was going to be my best chance of trying to get Nathaniel to stay. I needed to convince him that Nathaniel was better off with us.

At the first hearing everyone greeted me, and I tried to be as cordial as possible to each of them. (A little kissing up never hurt anybody!) I sat in one of the chairs that lined the back wall, approximately six feet behind the two curved tables. When the judge entered, one of the first things he did was to ask for introductions, for the record. Jack Day introduced me. Throughout the hearing I tried to lock eyes with the judge. I hoped that if I did, he would somehow be able to understand why I was here. I was admittedly trying to influence him. I thought my attendance would send him a message. The judge never looked in my direction, not even once!

As a matter of fact, once the hearing started nobody paid any attention to me. If I thought that I could somehow be involved just by showing up, I was sadly mistaken. I came in boldly, but I was feeling pretty feeble right about now. *"What am I going to do!?! Please God! Please let me have an opportunity to talk to the judge!"* One thing I can do is talk! My mother-in-law says that it takes me five minutes just to draw a breath. I just knew that if I could bend the judge's ear for just a minute, I could convince him to let Nathaniel stay. The hearing ended quickly, and I left feeling as though I didn't have a friend in the world. When the hearing began, I realized that there was nothing I could really do. I didn't have a right to be involved because he had not been in our home for twelve consecutive months.

"Oh please, God! Please postpone the hearing until Nathaniel has been in our home for twelve months! Please!!"

There were hearings that took place between January and June. During this time I got to meet James, the uncle that wanted to take custody of Nathaniel. He came up from Tennessee for almost every hearing, and Social Services would try to arrange for him to see Nathaniel every time he came up, much to our dismay. When he came up the first time we invited him over to our house to meet Nathaniel. Bonnie and I offered to let him come to the house because we thought that it would be less stressful for Nathaniel. But that wasn't the only reason. We knew that James was going to get a visit no matter what we said. And we didn't want him to be taken down to the Social Services office for the visit. I couldn't stand the thought of my boy being taken anywhere without Bonnie or me being with him. I also hoped that if James could see how happy Nathaniel was that maybe I could convince him to let him stay with us. We had James over at our house several times. In fact, one of the hearings fell on Nathaniel's birthday, March 15th. And we invited James to come to our house to celebrate.

It was a bittersweet celebration. I gave Nathaniel a big piece of chocolate cake and turned away from him to talk with his uncle. I was videotaping as well. When I turned around Nathaniel had chocolate frosting all over his face! Apparently he had decided to forgo using his hands, and he dove into the cake face first…he looked as if he had had a chocolate bomb explode all over his face…. You should have seen the puzzled looked that Nathaniel had! I was laughing on the outside, but inside my heart ached when I thought that maybe this would be the first and the last birthday that we would celebrate with him.

"Oh God! Please! Save my boy!!"

One night Bonnie went shopping. We live in the suburbs about a half hour out of town. By the time she came back I had put all the kids to sleep and was watching something on the television.

(The time just before we went to bed was probably the worst time for me throughout this ordeal. Especially when Bonnie was shopping and I found myself alone. I would often find myself in prayer and Bible study, which may sound good but as I was studying and praying my mind would be racing with scenarios of what it would be like to hand over Nathaniel to someone else.... The one thought that kept me from mentally falling apart was the belief that I was not alone. God knew my situation. *"He has never let me down and I don't expect that He's going to start now!"* I would constantly repeat to myself. I didn't **feel** as though God was with me but I had learned long ago that having faith in God is more of an act of the intellect than the heart (emotion).

I was hanging on by a slim thread. It's not good to be alone when battling depression and doubt.) This is the frame of mind I was in when Bonnie came home.

She was showing me what she bought when she pulled out this stuffed animal. It was blue and had long ears, like a beagle. It was made out of some material that made it cuddly soft. She said, "I bought this for Nathaniel. If he's going to leave, I want him to have this so that he can remember us by it. It even plays a tune. Squeeze it!" She threw me the dog, and I gave it a squeeze. There were no words, but I immediately recognized the tune that it played: "You are my sunshine, my only sunshine...." My mind immediately raced to the last words of that tune... "Oh please, don't take my sunshine away!"

Immediately I saw a picture in my mind. I saw a darkened room with a crib against one of the walls. The door to the room was slightly opened, allowing a sliver of light to come into it. This shard of light was falling on the crib. In the crib I saw Nathaniel, sitting up, crying for his mommy and daddy. The noises coming from the outside of the room told me that no one was coming to his aid. No one was paying attention. In the crib was that little stuffed dog playing that horrible tune. Outside the room I could hear the sound of people talking, enjoying themselves...while my son was crying and heartbroken in that little wooden prison. If someone had plunged a dagger into my chest it wouldn't have hurt as much as it did to see that vision. That is what would happen to Nathaniel if he were sent to live with the Johnsons.

I have never touched my wife except in love. I have never, and would never hurt my wife. But that night... I could not believe that she would buy that stupid, ugly, worthless piece of junk! I threw that dog back at her. I didn't hit her with it, but she was surprised at how hard I chucked it.

"What in the world is your problem?" she said. She had not thought about the words to the tune. She just liked it because it was soft and cute. I think she thought I had just lost my mind.

"Take that piece of garbage out of my sight!! I never want to see that thing again!" I couldn't bring myself to tell her what I had just seen. It hurt too much! I was choked up with anger and the words just wouldn't come out. About five minutes later I guess Bonnie figured out why I was upset because she said, "Oh no! Oh Miguel, I'm sorry! I didn't know what the song was until just now." I think that during this time we had both been living in a sort of mental limbo. We were both trying to find ways to deal with what was going on. She loved Nathaniel as much as I did. I'm sure she could write her own memoir of this experience.

Around this time I had to go to one of the hearings for Nathaniel. I don't remember exactly what it was for but I remember that everyone was talking to James. and all the lawyers were conversing together on how to get this thing over with quickly. Nathaniel was just one of many children that they had on their docket. I got the impression that they thought of Nathaniel as just one more kid, whose case they needed to dispose of so they could move on. But this was no ordinary kid. This was MY KID!

Everyone seemed to be on James's side. No one said a word to me... I felt all alone! During the hearing one of the lawyers asked the judge to summarily rule that Nathaniel should be given to the Johnsons. All the lawyers were in agreement. All they needed was for the judge to make a ruling. In my heart I tried to cry out to the Lord. I wanted to ask Him to be with me, to comfort me. If Nathaniel was going to leave, then I needed strength, Bonnie needed strength! I tried to pray to Him as the trial was underway, but the words just wouldn't come out. For once in my life I was speechless! You have to know me to know how rare that is. In my soul the only thing I could say to God at that moment was *"...Please, don't take my sunshine away!"*

The judge felt that they needed to complete all the paperwork before he could make that ruling. He postponed the decision because of a technicality!

A Marathon Requires Endurance

Looking back, I realize that I was not alone during those times. And as a matter of fact, God was working the whole time that I felt that He had left us to fend for ourselves. Nathaniel had been receiving chiropractic care because of the curvature of his neck. We had been taking him there ever since he had come to live with us. One evening when I was at the chiropractor's, I saw a familiar face. It was Jack Day, the lawyer for Social Services. He used the same chiropractor that we did. What a coincidence! I saw him, but I didn't say anything to him. He was on the other side of the office. And besides, I didn't want to make him feel as though he had to talk to me. To my surprise, Jack came over to us and said "Hi." Nathaniel was outside in the car with Bonnie; my older boys were being seen by the chiropractor also. John asked where Nathaniel was, and I said "outside with his mother."

"Good!" he said. "Well, you certainly have some good looking kids!" and looking at my older boys he asked, "How do you like having your little brother?" they just nodded. After that he said goodbye and left.

"That was strange! I've been coming here for seven months at the same time and have never seen him here before. And he referred to Nathaniel as their little brother. What's up with that?" I wondered if God was giving me a ray of hope that He was still working things out…. When I went outside, Bonnie told me that someone in a Mercedes drove by our van very slowly and was peering in as they went by. I didn't know what to make of it.

Although we knew that we could not get legally involved, I consulted a lawyer to find out just what our rights really were. Bonnie made some inquiries and found that there was one lawyer whose name kept popping up. Everyone she spoke with had nothing but praise for the man. His name was Keith Graham. Keith was a very professional yet affable attorney. When I spoke with him I felt as though I were his only client. I was very impressed. I explained to him my situation, and he bluntly told me that there was really nothing he or I could do. If I could somehow postpone these proceedings until after July 27th, then Bonnie and I could get legally involved and be considered by the judge as a possible placement for Nathaniel. The way the case was progressing, it seemed impossible to make it beyond July. Everyone expected that Nathaniel would be gone by April, or May. He did say to me, however, that I was very lucky to have David Packer as Nathaniel's law guardian. He advised me to speak with him and see if he could help me. So I made an appointment with Nathaniel's law guardian.

Bonnie and I both had misgivings about Nathaniel's aunt and uncle. We did not think it was in Nathaniel's interests to be placed with them. Something just didn't seem right. The first time that I met Nathaniel's uncle he seemed nice enough, but there were a couple of things that bothered me. The first was the way our first meeting ended when he came over our house. (I was always straight with him. I told him that we loved Nathaniel and that we wanted him to stay. I made all sorts of promises of keeping in touch with them and even of adopting them into our family if they would let Nathaniel stay. I must have sounded pretty desperate to him.) James looked at me as he was about to leave, and his eyes began to tear up. I knew what he was thinking…he knew that Nathaniel was better off with us. He knew that we truly loved him, and I think he somehow was mentally placing himself in our position. But something was holding him back from saying what was on his mind. I felt that he wanted to let Nathaniel stay but that there was something else going on that he couldn't seem to get out.

My second misgiving was that on one visit he stated that one of his concerns was keeping Nathaniel accessible to the biological parents. I didn't understand this. The judge had ruled that the biological parents were to have no contact with Nathaniel. What exactly were the Johnson's planning on doing? A conversation that Bonnie had with James' wife, Rose, told us what they were planning. Rose did not come up for any of the court dates because she had to take care of her own children. However, she called our house once a week or so to talk with Bonnie and check on Nathaniel. During one of those conversations Rose told Bonnie that their plan was to return Nathaniel to his biological mother once they get custody of him. Bonnie reminded her of the Judge's ruling, and she made a statement about waiting awhile to see if the mother "got her act together." Bonnie couldn't believe her ears! As was her custom, she immediately called me and told me what had gone on…. Now the situation was more serious. These people wanted to return Nathaniel to the bleak situation that the system was trying to save him from. They may have thought that they were doing a good deed, helping out Rose's sister-in-law, but they were in essence sentencing Nathaniel to a life of poverty, crime, and who knows what else. If Nathaniel was returned to those people, he might be back in front of another judge someday, but for something he had committed. We had to do something!

I spent quite a bit of time with James…he really was a nice guy. I obviously disagreed with him, but we really weren't that different. He had five children: I had four (with Nathaniel). He told me that he was a Christian: so was I. He wasn't a bad person, (I'm not too bad either) he just didn't have Nathaniel's best interest in mind. But it wouldn't have mattered. If the Pope and Mother Theresa had come forward to take custody of our son, we still would've believed there was something wrong with them. We were looking for reasons to find them unfit to take Nathaniel, and thank the Lord they gave us one. I had made an appointment with the Law Guardian, but I didn't know exactly what I would say to him… I had to do something!

A Ray of Hope!?!

I had spoken with Mr. Packer once or twice at the different court appearances, but only briefly; and whenever James was there he would greet him and tell him how great he thought it was that his family had come forward for Nathaniel. I admit being jealous that everyone smiled and paid attention to James, while I sat, alone, on the back row of chairs in the courtroom, seemingly without a friend in the world! —I know now that when I was there I was never truly alone.

Before I walked into his office I remember praying in my car that the Lord would move on this man to allow him to understand my situation. I was told by my lawyer that the information I have about the Johnsons' could be understood differently by different people, so I might be seen by the Law Guardian as someone grasping for straws. If Dave Packer didn't find my information important or trustworthy, then I would be back at Square One. Which meant I would be nowhere.

When I walked into his office, I was ushered into a large conference room on the second floor. The walls were lined with bookshelves that had legal books dating back to the beginning of recorded legal history, or so it seemed to me. When Mr. Packer came in he had a notepad with him, and I began my memorized speech… "Hi! My name is Miguel Crespo; I want Nathaniel to remain a member of my family. I believe that if he leaves our family and is taken to Tennessee, his best interests will not be served… I cannot be legally involved, as you know, until Nathaniel has been in our home for twelve months, but we are worried about what might happen to him…." I was nervous; I wanted to make my argument clear, but I was also trying to keep from sounding like some hysterical father, trying desperately to keep his son. Even though that was exactly what I was. I thought

38

that I would have to spend some time working on him, trying to get him to see things my way.

The meeting had lasted approximately five minutes when he looked at me and said, "Let me see…, now what could I do to extend this trial beyond those twelve months…?"

I just about fell over in my chair! After several more minutes of conversation he said,

"Look, I don't know you. I'm taking you at your word that what you're telling me is true. I'm going to be sticking my neck out for you, and I don't even know you! When the time comes and the judge asks me for my recommendation, I will tell him about these things. I can't promise you anything, but the judge takes the recommendation of the Law Guardian very seriously. As for the twelve months, there is really nothing I can do about that…the only thing I can tell you is that when the time comes I will give you an opportunity to take the stand and tell the judge the same thing that you just told me."

"That's more than I had hoped for! Thank you!" I was so happy I wanted to hug him, but I didn't think that would be proper.

As I left his office I remember walking down the stairs, almost euphoric. The kind of state a boy is in when he kisses a girl for the first time. "I can't believe it!" I said over and over as I approached my car; "That was great!!" When I finally sat in my car, it was then that I heard that familiar voice… *"Oh ye of little faith…"* I had believed that God had placed me in this situation; I believed that it was God's will that Nathaniel stay. I prayed that God would touch the heart of David Packer, and now that God had answered my prayer, my response was, "I can't believe it." What a dope! A true act of faith is to believe that God will answer even though every earthly sign points to the opposite. I believed that God wanted Nathaniel to stay, but because I hadn't heard anything since this whole thing started, I believed that God had somehow changed His mind. I think deep down inside we all have this concept of God being fickle. Or maybe it's just me? I interpreted his silence as a change of mind, or evidence of presumption on my part.

The truth is that God never changes. If He wants something to come to pass, He will bring it to fruition, regardless of the circumstances. I wonder if the times that it seemed God was silent in my life were the times that He couldn't take time to talk with me because He was too busy working on my behalf? Or maybe it was a test to see if I could walk by faith. I was beginning to learn what faith was really about. For the last few months I had been walking by faith, not really knowing if God had heard my prayers. I didn't know if Nathaniel was going to stay, but I at least knew that God would give us an opportunity to finally talk to the judge. I had no promises made, but at least I had something material to grasp onto. Now it was my turn to call Bonnie with some news. I found out as I was gathering my notes a year later that as I was speaking with the Law Guardian, Bonnie was praying at home for my success. The Bible says that the "effectual fervent prayer of a righteous man (in this case, woman) availeth much. James 5:16.

My newly resurrected faith was soon to take a hit. And to my shame I totally forgot about the event at the offices of Dave Packer. We, Bonnie and I, believed that we should share the same information that we had given Mr. Packer with the Case Worker. I thought that she would see things in the same light and finally try to help us keep Nathaniel. I couldn't have been more wrong! When Bonnie told her about what was going on she, very coldly replied that she didn't think that it would change the outcome. Nathaniel would still be given over to them. She spent very little time "digesting" the information. She just let it fly right past her as if it was no big deal. It was almost as if she didn't believe us. (I really, really didn't like her!) I began to think that maybe this was all some cruel joke. I had thought this meant that Nathaniel would stay, but after hearing about what the Case Worker said, I felt as if someone had let the air out of my balloon.

It was during times like these that I found myself struggling with God. A part of me wanted to give up. *"Just curse God and leave the church!"* I would sometimes be tempted to think. I thought about taking my family and moving to some far-off island. I had heard stories of how couples had adopted children, or taken in children, and then had to turn the children over to some undeserving biological relative. I had never thought in a million years that I would be one of those people. There were times when Bonnie and I would be watching the news and they showed a family giving their baby up to someone, amid the clicking and bright flashes of the news cameras. I would often tell Bonnie that I didn't understand how they could just turn their child over. "If it were me, I would just run away!" I would tell her. "There is no way I would turn my baby over to anybody!" And now here I was, in a similar situation. I thought about running away. But as much as I loved Nathaniel I had to think about my other kids as well. It wouldn't be fair to them. I couldn't make Bonnie and me fugitives because it would affect more than just the two of us. But I wouldn't be honest if I didn't say that I thought about kidnapping Nathaniel. Maybe that sounds shocking to hear from a theology major. Oh well....

I am so thankful for the church to which I belong. I thank God for the example that has been set for me by my "mothers and fathers" in the faith. Their prayers and support throughout that time were greatly appreciated. I learned from them how to face the storms of my life. Many times, when I felt close to the breaking point, I would fall on my knees, praying to God. I would open up my heart to Him. I would also open up the Scriptures and read. It didn't matter what the book or the chapter was, I would just read. I learned to do this because of the example of my church family.

Reading the Bible can be compared to mining for gold. You can spend hours digging away, trying to find that mother lode of inspiration, more precious than rubies, or gold. Sometimes I would find that elusive vein of gold. That spiritual manna that would feed and strengthen my weary, achy soul. Other times I would be reading the Scriptures and feel like I was hip deep in mining ore, vainly searching for what the devil kept telling I would never find. There were two Scriptures that were especially meaningful to me. The first in Psalms 84:11: "For the Lord God is a sun and shield; the Lord will give grace and glory; no good thing will he withhold from them that walk uprightly." Verse 12 states, " O Lord of hosts, blessed is the man that trusteth in thee." The reason that I appreciated that scripture so much was that the first time I read it, it seemed as if King David was talking directly to me. He was telling me that I could trust in God. God wants the best for me. Sometimes what I think is beneficial to me really isn't. I need to trust that God knows best.

Because of this the tone of my prayers began to change. Before this, I guess you could say that the primary thrust of my prayer was that God would let Nathaniel stay, and if Nathaniel was going to leave then I wanted to ask Him for the strength to continue. As the months dragged on, the theme of my prayers was more that God would perform His will in this situation, and give me the courage to accept whatever He chose. I still wanted Nathaniel to stay, but I began to think that maybe I was presuming a bit. If God did not want Nathaniel in our home, I knew better then to try and fight Him. I was beginning to see that it was going to take a miracle to keep Nathaniel in our home.

The other scripture that I found encouraging was Matthew 19:26. Bonnie came across this one during one of her devotions. As I understand it, she was reading the Bible when she came across this verse, and it seemed as if it was answering some unspoken prayer in her heart. One interesting thing about spending time with the Lord is that you can be reading the Scriptures, not looking for anything in particular, and then you come across a verse that helps you with some issue that has been broiling in the back of your mind. The Lord knows what we need, and if we let Him, He will lead us to the 'mother lode' I was referring to earlier. The verse states, "But Jesus beheld them, and said unto them, With men this is impossible; but with God all things are possible." I liked my verse better because it didn't seem so presumptuous, but I never told Bonnie that. I didn't have enough faith to believe Jesus' own words.

I had a dream one night. I debated whether or not to include this part because I don't know if it's relevant or not. In my heart I believe it is. Throughout the months leading up to the final court date I had been up and down emotionally. There were things that had happened that made me believe that Nathaniel was staying and things that led me to believe that we would lose him. I include this because it happened and it is something I will never forget.

In my dream I woke up in my house, it was pitch black, all the lights were out, except for the moonlight, which shined in from the mini-bay window. I found that darkness rather unusual because we usually leave a light on for the kids to find the bathroom. Without a light to see by it's easy to walk into a wall or something. Maybe the nightlight was for me?

Anyway, I walked into the living room, and in this darkness I noticed a man standing there, he was very tall. I couldn't make out his features because it was so dark but the way the moonlight fell on his face I could tell the features were masculine. It was a man, or a very tall, very ugly woman. The man said something to me that sounded like "He's coming" or, " It's coming…" I looked back towards the kitchen, where he intimated that "He" was coming from and noticed a small light, like the light of a flashlight. As the light came closer it began to get larger. I realized that this wasn't a flashlight, but rather a ball of light coming towards me. The ball of light came closer and closer, and kept getting larger and larger, I became afraid at that point. Even though the sphere of light got larger, the room was still enshrouded in darkness. I couldn't see anything but the light. As the light came right towards me I became so afraid that I assumed the fetal position, just as I was swallowed up by the light.

The next thing I knew, I was inside an old Jeep Cherokee. The kind with the fake wood paneling on the side, and the nose of the vehicle sharply pointing forward. I realized that I was in the Jeep, going down a gravel country road. I could hear the gravel crunching underneath the tires of the car. I knew I was dreaming so I just looked out the window as the car, seemingly by itself, went down the road. There was a grassy field on the left, and on the right there was a pasture, marked out by old split cedar posts, topped with barbed wire. *"Must be for horses."* I thought. There was a bend in the road up ahead and I thought about grabbing the wheel and steering away from the pasture. *"No, this is a dream... I've always wanted to do this. If I crash in a dream, will I get hurt? Will the car steer itself if I don't play along with the dream?"* I waited until the car was at the corner and almost on top of the barbed wire fence before I instinctively grabbed the wheel and jerked it away from it. *"Is this a dream? That felt so real!"* I drove the car the rest of the way down the gravel road.

After awhile I realized that it wasn't a road that I was driving on, but a driveway. I looked ahead and saw that the driveway led up to two houses that were side by side. The homes were out in the middle of an open field. Aside from the fence and the two houses there were no signs of civilization. It was beautiful. Both houses were two story, single family homes. They were similar to the kind you would find in any middle class neighborhood. *"I wonder who lives in those houses?—Oh great! Which house do I pull into? And what do I tell the people when they ask what I'm doing here?"* Just then I saw Bonnie come out of the home on the right. It looked as if she came out to tend the flowers. Instinctively I guided the car into that driveway. *"This is my house?"* I was confused, big time! When I parked the car I got out and went around the car to see Bonnie. When I came up to her I noticed that there was someone next to her. It was Nathaniel, he had followed Bonnie outside. Both of them looked as if they didn't have a care in the world. *"This must mean that Nathaniel is going to stay!"* Just then I was suddenly pulled back into the real world. I woke up. I wish I could've stayed asleep forever.

Was that a sign from God? Had I been thinking about this so long that it affected my dreams? Maybe I shouldn't have had that bean burrito before I went to bed? I don't know. Part of my college class work that semester was studying the life, and visions of the prophetess, Ellen G. White. Maybe I had subconsciously jumbled all my thoughts together and came up with that dream? One day I hope to find out the truth.

The Final Countdown: Are you ready?

May 24, 2002—one more hearing in the long line of hearings. I, as usual, showed up and sat behind the two curved tables, and spent the time before the hearing in silent prayer. There were two petitions that Judge Lawless had to deal with throughout this ordeal. One was the petition by the biological parents of Nathaniel to get custody. And the other was the petition of the aunt and uncle to be given custody of him. The bio-family had figured that if they approached the court from both angles, one of them would likely win out; and they would still get what they wanted, Nathaniel. Now the judge had already ruled that Nathaniel would not go to either of the biological parents; however they still had the right to challenge that ruling and try and get him to reverse it. On this day I thought the judge would hand over Nathaniel to someone other than Bonnie and me. We had been going around and around since January, that was five months ago. The longest five months of my life.

At the hearing the lawyers expected that the judge would give custody to the aunt and uncle. James Johnson was there that day. Everyone thought that the bio-parents' petition would be thrown out, especially because neither one had shown up to any of the earlier court dates. And that day was no exception. The judge asked for introductions and the lawyers for the bio-parents informed the judge that, as usual they had not been able to contact either one of them but that in their last conversations with them they had expressed their desire to have Nathaniel returned to the biological mother. I felt bad for the lawyers. They basically were trying to put lipstick on a pig. The judge promptly disposed of the matter by denying their petition for custody for lack of interest. While I was happy at the outcome, I knew that that was going to be the easy one.

All the lawyers were in agreement that day that Nathaniel should go to live with the Johnsons. I didn't realize this then but before the lawyers appear before a judge they usually get together and discuss what they are going to do. It almost seems as though the actual hearing is just a formality because they have decided beforehand what they are going to do. Well, they had decided that they would ask the judge to grant custody to the Johnson family. The only sticking point was that the paperwork for the homestudy that was done for the Johnsons had not been officially received yet. According to the Case Worker, the completed forms had been mailed from Tennessee but were stuck at the Albany, New York office. Praise the Lord for red tape! She had tried to get them to fax the judge a copy, but they couldn't find the paperwork to do that. But according to the Case Worker, the homestudy had been completed, and the Johnsons had been approved. They all hoped that the judge would accept their recommendation and allow them to tie up the paperwork after the fact.

When the issue of the home study came up before the judge, he ruled that the custody hearing would have to be moved to another date to allow for the paperwork to come in. *"Whew!!"* I thought. That was just another bullet in a long line of bullets that we (Bonnie and I) had dodged. The judge looked at his calendar and finally said, "How does June 12th sound to you, Mr. Johnson? I know it's a long way from Tennessee, but we are almost at the end. Will that date work for you?" James agreed on the date, and all the lawyers marked their calendar: June 12, 2002. Barring a miracle, Nathaniel would be leaving us on that day. Even though I felt a heaviness in my heart, I had this feeling – *"Nathaniel is my son. God won't let him be taken from me."* I can only explain what I felt inside as a struggle. Part of me wanted to become hysterical and start crying, and the other part was telling me to wait, wait and see what the Lord was going to do. I decided that if I was going to break down and get hysterical, I would wait until I knew for sure what was going to happen. I called Bonnie and told her about the date.

This Is My Boy!

My heart ached when I thought about Nathaniel. He was at home right now, playing and running around the house, totally unaware that in a few weeks his whole life was going to be turned upside down. No child deserves that.

The Breaking Point

Throughout the previous six months Bonnie and I had tried to maintain a normal schedule. We went to church every Sabbath; I was regularly involved in my church as an Elder, I also had the privilege of preaching once a month at one of our sister churches. We tried to attend all the church events in spite of the fact that we may not have always felt like going. On this particular Sabbath the services were being held at Camp Cherokee. Cherokee is a summer camp nestled in the Adirondack Mountains in Upstate New York, little more than a 45 minute ride from my house. It's a beautiful place, right on the lake, and it has been a place where many summer campers have come to know the Lord for the first time. Every year the churches in our Northern Adirondack District come together to fellowship with each other. Because of the distance between our churches we don't see each other very often so this gives the members an opportunity to visit the camp, and each other, and enjoy a Sabbath together. It's usually an all-day event. They even encourage people to come up on Friday and spend the night. I usually don't stay all day because my allergies start to act up after awhile. Besides, Saturday nights are when I get together with my friends to play Basketball. And the truth be told, I would rather play basketball with my friends. So every year some of us guys mysteriously disappear from the camp on Sabbath afternoon and go back home so we can be ready for sundown, and for basketball.

On that Sabbath day there seemed to be people visiting who were not members of any of the churches in our district. I'm not even sure if they were Adventists. I remember a group of them sitting on lounge chairs on the dock. They seemed to be oblivious to us locals, going back and forth from Sabbath School, to the cafeteria, and back to the chapel. They were city folk on vacation, by the looks of them. By the way they were lying in their seats they looked like they had only one thing on their minds: rest and relaxation.

Even though we were about a week and a half away from D-day (June 12th), I don't remember being particularly nervous or worried about it. I knew the day was getting closer, but I didn't spend a whole lot of time thinking about it that day. I think I was just trying to enjoy the time that I had with Nathaniel. With all the highs and lows I had been through in the last half year, I had gotten pretty adept at not letting anything get past that mental barrier that I had set up. I was also holding onto the hope that Nathaniel would stay.

Even though our church family knew what we were going through, and knew that the date was fast approaching, no one said anything to us that day. It was just as well. My church family is full of wonderful people, but they stink when it comes to providing comfort. I remember speaking with several different people throughout this ordeal and remember how horrible their advice was. One good friend told me that maybe it was part of God's plan for Nathaniel to leave. It could be that maybe the Johnsons would take Nathaniel and after a few months they might realize that he's better off with us. Then maybe I would be able to get him back.

"Oh great, Just what I wanted to hear! Let's stretch this nightmare out even more! Just when I begin to come to grips with losing my son, they want to give him back."

I know he was trying to help, but he didn't. Another member told me that we should ask God to let His will be done and just accept it. —I knew all of these things. Did they think that they were providing comfort to me? If anything, they were depressing me. After a while I became so annoyed with their so-called comforting words that I just stopped talking to my friends about it. The only person that could understand what I was going through was the only other person that was going through the same thing, my wife. The sad irony is that I was giving that same annoying advice to my wife throughout this whole experience. I wish I had a dime for every time that I told my wife that we needed to ask the Lord for His will to be done. I wish I had a dollar for every time that I tried to explain to her different scenarios that might play out. I thought I was helping her, but I wasn't. Sometimes truth gets in the way of giving comfort to a hurting soul.

I remember talking with her one night, as we usually did. We were talking about something her mother had told her. She was trying to encourage Bonnie, but how do you cheer someone up who is in danger of losing her child forever? I remember telling Bonnie how she shouldn't let what people say get her down.

"Hey, opinions are like armpits, OK? We all have at least two, and they all stink!" I tried to cheer her up.

She chuckled and said, "You know what? I don't want people to tell me what they think, or how we should trust in the Lord. I already know that! I just want someone to tell me that everything's gonna be all right."

Truer words have never been spoken. I knew all the things that my friends were telling me. I didn't need a lecture on trusting God! I'm majoring in theology for Pete's sake! I just wanted to be told that everything was going to be all right. I didn't need logic, or reasoning, but a reassuring hug, and a simple, "Don't worry Man, God will work things out." Somehow, someway, He would take care of me. As I thought about that, it dawned on me that I had done that very same thing that I complained about in others with my wife. I tried to apply Scripture and reasoning to allay her fears, but what she needed most was just someone to tell her that everything was going to be all right. *"I stink at giving comfort and advice too."* I put my arms around her and hugged her, and told her, "Don't worry, Babe, everything is going to be all right."

I've learned that when people are hurting—it doesn't matter the situation—they don't need logic, or reason. Those things are important and have their place, but what does the most good when someone is hurting is just being there. Give that person a

This Is My Boy!

52

Make me a servant, humble and meek
Lord, let me lift up those who are weak
And may the prayer of my heart always be
Make me a servant, make me a servant
Make me a servant today.

As all the beautiful voices in that chapel blended together in perfect harmony, I closed my eyes and allowed the perfect blending of harmony and truth to fill my soul. That song was my prayer to God.

As we were in the middle of the song I suddenly heard a voice in my head say, *"If you love Me, you have to let Nathaniel go! Do you love Me?"* It was clear, unmistakable. I had not even been thinking about Nathaniel at the time. The voice was powerful, unequivocal, and gentle and subdued, all at the same time. Finally, I lost it, I knew then that I was going to lose my son! I picked up my sleeping, 14-month-old baby boy and rushed out of that room, tears streaming down my face. It was as if the levee had broken; I couldn't stop the tears, I tried to suck up the tears running down my face but it was no use; I was out of control. That same voice kept repeating in my head, *"Do you love Me? You have to let him go!"*

This was the breaking point for me. I had put my trust in God and refused to let any negative thoughts into my head. I would not consider even for a moment that my son might be taken from me. But this... God had spoken to me! I had to decide; do I trust God completely or not? If God allows my son to be taken from me, will I still serve Him? Worship Him? Love Him? If I loved God, I had to let Nathaniel go.... Did I love God?

There is a porch on the side of the chapel that faces the lake. Since the chapel is on a slope, which leads down to the lake, there are stairs near the chapel that go down to the dock. When I ran out of the chapel I first sat on one of the chairs on the porch. I tried to get myself together... I'm a grown man, I shouldn't be crying like some big baby. I tried to turn off my tears but they just would not stop coming. My face was soaking wet. I looked down at Nathaniel. He was still sleeping, even though I had almost leaped out of my chair and run out. I walked down the length of the porch with Nathaniel in my arms and sat at the top step of the stairs that led to the dock. I could hear the voices of the other visitors at the camp. There were four or five of them sitting on lounge chairs down on the dock. We were separated by about forty feet and they couldn't see me because of the brush in between, so I just sat there and cried my eyes out, thinking about what I had just heard in my head.

After about five minutes I calmed down enough to stop crying. I had no idea that the tear glands could create so much water so quickly. As I sat there contemplating my answer to God, I rehearsed in my mind all the different times that God had been there for me. I thought about the time I thought about ending my life because I thought life was unbearable. I thought about how God had sent someone to talk with me that day, and how he told me that Jesus had the antidote for what was ailing me. I remember when I turned around to say something to him (in our conversation he told me his name was Michael) and found that he had disappeared... I knew that God loved me. What was I going to do? I thought about God's love, and his protection over me and my family over the years. I remembered the time that Jacob (he was three years old at the time) opened the rear car door of our Isuzu Rodeo while my wife was driving. She swerved the vehicle, and when she did so the car headed for the woods, so she had to swerve back, which threw Jacob with even more force into the unlocked door. I remember her telling me that Jacob didn't fall out. But when she stopped the car and went to the back door to open it, she found that it was unlocked, and the door swung freely open. God's angels had worked overtime that week. For you see, a few days later Bonnie was driving home in a severe rainstorm and hydroplaned into the woods on the side of the road. Aside from a scratch on the vehicle, everyone was fine. Had the vehicle traveled another six inches she would have hit a tree. God had given me many reasons to know and believe that He was alive and well in my life.

As I contemplated all these things I knew what my answer had to be. I put one hand behind Nathaniel's head and neck and the other hand under his bottom, and I said, "Lord, I love Nathaniel, but I love you more! If You want him, take him; he's Yours." I lifted up Nathaniel over my head and held him up to God. He wasn't mine anymore. If God believes that Nathaniel is better off somewhere else, then let the Lord's will be done. The tears began to flow again. And at that moment I felt a peace come over me that can only be compared with receiving anesthesia just before an operation. It was a supernatural peace. A peace that spoke, *"Don't worry; everything's gonna be all right!"* I don't have to tell you that that was one of the hardest things I have ever done in my life. It's easy to do God's will when things are going your way.

June 9, 2002

There were just a few days until Nathaniel was scheduled to leave. The Case Worker had called Bonnie and told her that she had been in contact with the Johnsons. Their plan was to come up from Tennessee the day before the custody hearing and come to our house to visit Nathaniel for a few hours. The day of the hearing they would take Nathaniel for the afternoon, and the day after that they would take Nathaniel with them, forever. I decided that I wanted to do something to keep Nathaniel's memory alive. I decided that I wanted to put his handprint in cement so that we would have it, and never forget him.

Several years earlier Bonnie and I had built an addition onto our house, and when I had the cement poured I had some left over. Bonnie and I decided that we would use the leftover cement to make a little walking path to the electric meter box. I couldn't think of anything else to use it for, so we had the cement guy pour it and I shaped it into a semi-straight path. Before the cement hardened I had all of the family come out and place their left hands into the cement. I thought it would be nice to look back on. It would be really cool, I thought, when they get older and compared their hands with what they were like when they were kids. I remember telling Bonnie, "I hope we never have to move. How am I going to get that thing up out of there?"

I thought that it would be a good idea to put Nathaniel's handprint alongside the rest of our prints. *"They may take Nathaniel away, but they will never take away his memory!"* I thought to myself. I had to use my Skil saw and a mason blade to cut lines into the concrete. I marked out the spot that I was going to use with the saw. When I had made my cuts, I began to hammer out the pieces of cement that were in between the lines that I had scored. It seemed like a good idea at the time, but apparently the cement didn't think so. It fought me all the way. First, it resisted the blade so that I had a hard time cutting into it. Second, it wouldn't let go of the pieces I tried to hammer out without a fight. Every time I whacked the cement with my hammer it would spit back at me. I had safety glasses on as I remember but that didn't seem to make a difference. I wasn't sure who was going to win, me or the cement. Eventually I was the victor, but my face showed the welts inflicted by the conflict.

I had bought a little bag of cement and began to mix it and pour it into the spot. When it was ready I had Bonnie bring Nathaniel out, and while she was holding his upper body, I lowered his left hand into the cement. As soon as his hand felt the wet cement, Nathaniel made a fist, and his handprint looked more like the depression made when someone sticks a chip into a bowl of bean dip. "That's not gonna work!" I said to Bonnie.

I really wanted to do this, but when Nathaniel scooped out the cement I thought that maybe I wasn't supposed to put his print alongside the rest of the family. This made me more determined. Bonnie mentioned something about maybe waiting for the cement to dry and I said, "It's dry enough! Don't worry about it." I added some more cement and told her not to go anywhere. She just stood there holding Nathaniel with drying cement on his hand. I smoothed the cement once more and decided that maybe it would be a better idea to put his footprint in the cement. That way he won't be able to dig at the cement as we lowered him into it. That didn't work either! When Nathaniel felt the cement he stiffened up and again dug a hole in the cement rather than leaving a print. Finally I came up with a bright idea, "I think I need to wait for the cement to dry." I looked over to Bonnie to see if she approved, and what a sight! Here was my wife, one hand holding Nathaniel by the left wrist, and the other holding him by the right calf. She was trying to keep Nathaniel balanced so he wouldn't fall, but also trying to keep the cement from spreading to her. With one eyebrow raised up and her mouth half opened in a snarl at me, I got the impression that she wasn't too enthused with my idea...I thought it was a good one. She took him inside to clean him up while I smoothed out the cement again and waited outside for it to harden a little. I thought it was safer outdoors. After ten minutes we brought Nathaniel out and placed his left footprint alongside the left handprints of the rest of the Crespo family.

This was my way of saying to the world: to the judge, the lawyers, the case worker, and maybe even to God (I admit this to my shame), that even though they were taking Nathaniel away from us, they could never take away his memory from us. I hoped that someday I could show Nathaniel his footprint and have him compare it to the size his foot would be when he was grown.

Something else happened in the days leading up to June 12th that I would like to share. As I stated before, our church family was very aware of what we were going through and they did try to find ways to help us. There was one in particular whom I appreciate very much. That person is Roger Windover. He is my wife's uncle, but I've come to regard him more as a father because of the way he and his wife have treated me over the years. Roger was the head elder of our church at the time. He is also the owner of the local hardware store. In his time in this town he has gotten to know a lot of people. One of the people he had gotten to know was Judge Lawless. Roger used to drive a school bus some years back, and one of the students that he daily drove to and from school was Judge Lawless. He wasn't a judge then, as I understand it he was just a teenager. But Roger swears that he got to know him pretty good in his time as a bus driver. What I share now was told to me by Roger himself.

Roger decided to write the judge a letter. Neither Bonnie nor I was aware of his intentions. In his letter to the judge he told him how much we loved Nathaniel and how happy Nathaniel was with us. He told him that we wanted to adopt him but that he hadn't been in our home for twelve months yet so we couldn't get legally involved. We were just forty-five days away. Now, writing the letter isn't as interesting as the trip the letter took to get to the judge.

Roger decided he didn't want to mail the letter, so he faxed it. The problem was that the fax machine he sent the letter to was not the fax for the family court but the fax for the Sheriff's office. When the fax reached the Sheriff's office, someone looked at it, saw the name 'Lawless', and automatically assumed that it was for the Sheriff. It was then promptly delivered into his office. The Sheriff for our county is the father of the judge who is in charge of Nathaniel's case! When the Sheriff read the letter, he called Roger at the hardware store and told him of his mistake in sending it to the wrong place. As they were speaking, the Sheriff told him that he thought that he had written a very touching letter and decided that Roger didn't need to refax the letter to the judge. He said, "Don't worry! I'm going to take this letter over to his office myself. And I will make sure that my son sees it!"

Roger was so excited as he shared that story with me. I was very grateful for his effort, but I admit that in the light of what had happened at Cherokee, I didn't get as jazzed up as he did. But I thanked God for someone who cared to do something truly useful, and comforting.

June 11, 2002

The days leading up to the 12th of June were tough ones. On the day before the hearing the Johnsons were supposed to come up from Tennessee to visit Nathaniel at our house. Social Services wanted to try to work things out so that it wouldn't be such a shock to Nathaniel to be taken away. —Yeah right! How ridiculous! I know that they were trying to make the best out of a bad situation, but I confess that I was angry. This was going to hurt that little boy.

It turned out that we never heard from Social Services that morning. They were supposed to call us and schedule a time for the Johnsons to visit our house, but they didn't call until the afternoon. When Angie Dow (the case worker) finally called, she said that she had just spoken to the Johnsons and that they were still in Tennessee. They would not be visiting Nathaniel today. Bonnie and I were glad that we had Nathaniel to ourselves for one more day and angry that these people thought so little of what taking Nathaniel away would do to him. There was a fire burning inside of me. First, they want to take away my son, and now this... I was starting to get really torqued off!

That night, as we gathered for prayer with our children, we all prayed that God would let Nathaniel stay. In my heart I prayed that if God allowed Nathaniel to go, then please give me the strength to keep this family together. It wasn't just Bonnie and I, and Nathaniel that would be devastated by this. I was also worried about my other children as well. Every night before we all went to bed I would pray with my children. I don't know exactly why, but we got into the habit of splitting up at night. I would pray with Joshua and Jacob in their room, and Bonnie would pray with Hannah in her room. The prayers of all of the kids would always be the same. "Please let Nathaniel stay." We are a praying family. Every morning we begin as a family with prayer, and every night we end it with prayer. Every time one of the children would pray to the Lord about allowing Nathaniel to stay, I would offer up a prayer of my own that God would honor their request. Not just for my sake, but for theirs. What's going to happen to their faith if they spend all these months asking God for something and then they don't get it? I worried about the impact that Nathaniel's leaving would have, not only on their little hearts, but also on their faith. I went to bed that night praying for a miracle, one way or the other....

June 12, 2002

I woke up that morning in a somber mood. I wasn't sad; I wasn't happy. I just wanted to get this thing over with. The one thing that I decided to do was to try and talk with the judge in the hopes that he would deny the Johnsons' request for custody. I hadn't forgotten what had happened at Camp Cherokee, but I also knew that I had to be true to myself. And I wasn't letting Nathaniel go without giving 110% at trying to keep him. The offer from Nathaniel's law guardian was still on the table. He was going to let us get up front and tell the judge what we knew about the Johnson's intentions. If the judge found us credible, then maybe we might stand a chance.

Bonnie and I had written down all the information that we wanted to relate to the judge. On the days leading up to this date we had gone over and over those papers, trying to memorize everything so that we wouldn't leave anything out. As I looked over the papers I realized that it really came down to how one interpreted the information. We had the benefit of not just hearing the words they said, but also hearing how they said it. And that makes a big difference. It could be that just sharing the information may not mean anything to the judge. It hadn't meant anything to the Case Worker.

I took the day off so that I could be with my family. The plan was to leave the children with my mother-in-law and Bonnie and I would go into town. I hoped that when we came back the Crespos would still be six in number. I remember stepping onto our small front porch that morning and looking out at all the trees that surrounded our property. We only had an acre, but there sure were a lot of trees. If these trees could talk they could tell you about all the struggles we had had in the last seven or eight months. A lot of the events took place in their presence. I thought about what it would be like to lose one of my kids. And I thought about what my attitude would be towards God because of it. Just then, almost without thinking about it, I began to sing a song:

Take up thy cross and follow me
I heard my Master say
I gave Myself to ransom thee
Surrender your all today
Wherever He leads, I'll go
Wherever He leads, I'll go
I'll follow my Christ who loves me so
Wherever He leads, I'll go

I started out singing, but by the end the words were coming out slow and soft. It was my way of letting God know that I was willing to follow. I know that He wants what's best for me. And although I didn't understand, and didn't necessarily agree with it, He's God, and I'm not. I had no choice but to obey.

Bonnie and I left the kids at Penny's (my mother-in-law) and headed to the city for the 9:30 a.m. hearing. I promised the kids that we would call when it was over. They weren't overly worried. You see, I hadn't told anyone about what had happened at Cherokee. And I was always positive with my kids. I constantly told them over and over that I believed God would let Nathaniel stay. Whenever any one of them began to doubt or question whether or not he would stay, I would point them to Christ. I would tell them that I believed God wanted him here. I know that I was setting myself up for quite a fall, if and when he left, but I truly believed that Nathaniel was meant to stay. I remember one time when my oldest boy, Joshua, and I were driving home from town. He looked at me and said, "Dad, why do you have more faith then the rest of us? Why do you think Nathaniel is going to stay?" He had overheard some of our conversations. He had an idea that the situation was very serious. I didn't waver in the slightest. I told him, "Josh, I believe God can do anything. God does miracles all the time. The very fact that I'm alive today is a miracle of God. God has never let me down. I know I can trust Him. I know I can trust Him!" I said it with conviction, but it was more to shore up my faith than his. I believe those kids fully expected that Nathaniel was going to stay, and that's why they weren't so concerned that morning.

The family court offices are located in the government building. This building also houses the Department of Motor Vehicles, the County Clerk, the Veterans Agency…it's always packed with people. When we got there I noticed that there were very few people there as I walked in. As a matter of fact, besides Bonnie and myself, there was maybe just one other person there. This, combined with the fact that we were a few minutes early, allowed us the opportunity to go over the information that we had typed out so that we could relay it to the judge. I didn't want to leave out anything. I felt as if I was cramming for a final exam. When we finished 'cramming,' we got into the elevator and went up to the floor that housed all of the court offices.

When we got to the third floor I again was stunned to see so few people in the hallways. Usually there are anywhere between fifty and one hundred people in the halls, waiting to go into the criminal, civil, or family courtrooms.

"Maybe someone called in a bomb threat? That would be great! Then they would have to postpone this hearing… If there's a bomb in here what am I doing here? What if they think we called in the bomb threat…? Maybe I should call in a bomb threat?"

These were just some of the thoughts running through my mind. *"Where are James and Rose Johnson?"* I walked over to the usual spot that Jim sat at when he came to visit, and he wasn't there. Including Bonnie and me there were probably ten people there that day. "Could it be possible that we got the time wrong for the hearing?" I said to Bonnie. She just shrugged her shoulders.

At 9:35 a.m. we finally saw the Case Worker exit the area where the court clerk's office was, and she came over to us. I admit that I was totally confused at this point. I had rehearsed a hundred different scenarios in my mind about how this hearing would go, but I admit that I didn't see this coming.

"They aren't here!" Angie said.

"What do you mean, they aren't here?" I was in shock!

"They missed their flight. They never came up."

"What! They only got one plane in Tennessee?" I was in shock, and now I was angry.

"They faxed a letter to the judge and told him they wouldn't be able to make it."

"Well, what does that mean?" I was angry, but I began to see that something good might happen out of this.

"It means that the judge will probably just postpone the custody hearing for a week or two."

"This is ridiculous! These people don't care at all about Nathaniel. If it was me, you would have to kill me to keep me from being here—" I had to stop talking. I was about to fly off the handle.

I didn't know what to think. I truly had no idea what was going to happen next. Bonnie looked at me. (When couples have been married for a while, they tend to develop the ability to speak to each other with just a look. Bonnie and I could have a whole conversation with just looks.) Bonnie raised her eyebrows and shrugged her shoulders; at the same time she turned over one of her hands to expose her palm. Her look said, "What is going to happen now?" I raised my eyebrows, shrugged my shoulders, and turned over both palms. My look said, "I don't have a clue!"

A few minutes later the lawyers came out of the court clerk's office, and we all entered the courtroom. Judge Lawless and all the lawyers assumed their usual positions. Present at the hearing were: Judge Lawless; Nathaniel's law guardian, David Packer; the Social Services lawyer, Jack Day; and Angie Dow. The Johnsons never bothered to hire an attorney throughout the process. All the other lawyers were working with him every time he came up, so he didn't think it necessary to go through the extra expense.

I had brought some blank paper with me because I wanted to record what happened at the hearing. But the hearing lasted all of five minutes, so I didn't have much to write. After the introductions, the Judge read the fax that the Johnsons had sent to him. The letter basically asked for the court's forgiveness and asked for a postponement of the hearing. They did not give any explanation for not making it to the hearing, and the judge also stated that they did not offer any proof that they had actually bought a ticket. In spite of all of this, the judge seemed not to think too badly of what they had done. His reaction told me that he was ready to overlook their mistake.

I was so disappointed! I didn't understand what was going on. *"If the Johnsons truly cared about Nathaniel they would be here. Can't the judge see that?"*

After reading the letter the judge said that he was disposed to grant the request of the Johnsons' to postpone the hearing to another day, but he wanted to hear from the lawyers what their thoughts were on this. The first up was the law guardian. Mr. Packer stood up and said, "Your honor, I believe it would be in Nathaniel's best interests if you dismiss the petition of the Johnsons', and if they want to pursue custody further then they can refile their paperwork with the court."

My jaw dropped! *"I can't believe it!"* Bonnie's grip tightened on my hand.

Judge Lawless next looked over to the lawyer for Social Services and asked him what he thought about the law guardian's recommendation. Jack Day stood up and said, "Your honor, I don't have any problem with that." My grip tightened on Bonnie's hand.

"Very well then, I hereby dismiss the petition of the Johnson family for custody of Nathaniel. I will make sure that we mail them a copy of the decision and they can take it from there. Thank you, everybody." With that, the judge stood up and left.

Although our hands were locked in a death grip you could have knocked us over with a feather. I looked around as the lawyers gathered their papers and closed up their briefcases. I wanted someone to explain to me what just went on here. It had happened way too fast. Just then the law guardian motioned for me and Bonnie to follow him outside into the hallway. It was there that I found out what had happened.

David Packer said to me, "When we went into the judge's chambers, he read to us the fax that the Johnsons had sent. He wanted to postpone the hearing, but I told him that you folks wanted to adopt Nathaniel. I suggested to him that he dismiss the Johnsons' petition and give you a chance to have Nathaniel in your home long enough to get legally involved. At that point he could look at the two families and decide which family would be better for Nathaniel. The judge agreed, and here we are. I don't know if the Johnsons will even file again. But if they do, the hearing won't take place for at least a few months. This will give you time to get a lawyer and file for custody yourselves. Good luck!" With that he shook my hand and went on his way.

"HALLELUJAH! PRAISE THE LORD!!!!" I could hardly contain myself. I looked at Bonnie with my eyes wide open and my mouth wide open. That means, "Can you believe it?"

How can I put into words the tremendous joy I felt at that moment…. Everything came down to that hearing. I saw a genuine miracle that day. And I learned an important lesson in faith too. I had seen the God of the universe at work. God worked things out according to His master plan, and I had a front row seat. I needed a miracle and God gave me one. Joy unspeakable! I would get to keep my son! —I saw the Case Worker as she left the courtroom. She didn't look too happy. It's not that she didn't want Nathaniel to stay; she now had more paperwork to do. With the dismissal of the petition, she still had to deal with Nathaniel's situation. One more child whose future she had to continue to look out for.

Imagine that you are a boxer contending for the heavyweight championship of the world. You spend months training, conditioning yourself for the battle. Finally the day comes for the fight. You step into the ring and face your opponent. As soon as the bell rings, you come out ready to do what you've prepared for all this time. All of a sudden your opponent trips on a shoelace, falls down, and knocks himself out. You win, TKO. As weird as that may sound, that is what that day felt like. I knew God had stepped in and performed a miracle that day.

I prayed a prayer of Thanksgiving like I had never prayed before. Bonnie told me that she had felt so sick that morning that she thought she would throw up. When she saw what happened in that courtroom, she was as surprised and excited as I was. I held her hand tightly as we left that courtroom for fear that she might start doing cartwheels down the hallway.

As we walked down the hallway and got on the elevator, I heard a voice in my head again. God spoke to me that day. It wasn't a message; it was more like random impressions that corresponded to the different thoughts that were racing through my mind.

"I told you that everything was going to be all right!"

"I don't need your help. You thought you needed to talk to the judge... I got it covered!"

I cannot express how happy I was at that moment! I could finally breathe again. I could enjoy the sunshine, I could hear the birds singing, I could taste the sweetness of the air. God cared about my situation! With an entire universe to run, God cared enough to find a home for Nathaniel, He cared enough to work things out to ensure that Nathaniel would not be taken from the place where He wanted him to be. Bonnie and I called my mother-in-law and told her the news…we could hear the kids cheering in the background. We hurried home to enjoy our family, without the sword of Nathaniel's uncertain future hanging over our heads.

We spent the rest of the day at home doing nothing in particular, except enjoying our time together. As I looked back on the months before this day, I realized that God had been testing me. I thought about a sermon that I had given at my church one Sabbath. It was about Abraham offering Isaac, or attempting to offer Isaac. He did so because God told him too. The sermon was about how unfair God seems at times. The point I tried to make was that sometimes God seems unfair, but if we could see the end from the beginning we would know that there is a reason for everything that God allows. In the middle of that sermon I said, "It was only when Abraham was truly ready to give up his son that God let him keep his son." As soon as the words were out of my mouth I had a thought that maybe it was the same situation for me.

I thought about the times when I felt so stressed that I thought about turning my back on the God whom I believed had abandoned me… *"How would this have turned out had I given up my faith in God?"* I thought about the needless worrying; in reality Nathaniel was never in trouble. I was allowing myself to get all worked up over something in the future. The Bible deals with the issue of worry. It counsels us to not worry about tomorrow; there is enough going on today. I saw that I needed to learn to lean more fully on God for my tomorrows. And I made a promise to myself that day to never doubt God again. I decided that I wanted to be a man of faith.

It was a great day! The night, however, could've used some improvement. Nathaniel stayed up until midnight, screaming, crying, and just being an all-around grump. As I held Nathaniel, trying to rock him to sleep, I looked over at Bonnie and scrunched up my nose and raised my right eyebrow higher than the left. That meant, "We went through all that, for this?" She just laughed. —Be careful what you wish for....

"It ain't over yet"

June 12th was very special in several different ways. Of course I was elated at the way things had turned out, but I also learned a great deal about myself, and about God. I learned a great deal about what real faith is. I also learned a lot about the kind of God that I serve. I also learned that June 12th was not the end of this issue, but just the beginning.

I visited Keith Graham and retained him as our lawyer. He seemed genuinely happy for us, but he told me that nothing was definite yet. There were a lot of issues that had to be dealt with before we could adopt Nathaniel. There was the issue of the termination of the parents' rights. The rights of the mother were terminated, but the biological father's rights had not been terminated yet. This was no big deal before June 12th, because everyone believed that Nathaniel would be turned over to the father's sister. Now with us in the picture, his rights would have to be terminated first. After that, there was the issue of the Johnsons' custody petition. Graham informed me that this could take at least a year to sort out because of all the complications. I didn't really care about that. The bottom line was that Nathaniel was home. And as far as I was concerned, all these issues were non-issues, because my God wanted Nathaniel to stay.

Retaining Graham was something that I didn't think twice about. Bonnie and I had discussed how we would pay him and we both agreed. We would do whatever we had to do to come up with the money for his services. We wanted the best. I've frequently told Bonnie that it would have been cheaper and less stressful for us if we had gone to China and adopted a child there. Except that we didn't want just any child, we wanted **this** child. A child whose name I had to change from 'Godzilla' to 'The King', because everything he wanted, he got.

I would come home from work and my wife would have a story to tell me of some misdeed of his…how he chased his sister around the house, whacking her on the head with one of her own dolls. I would listen to stories of how Nathaniel single-handedly hauled a chair all the way from the living room to Joshua and Jacob's room, and climbed over the barrier the older boys had created to keep Nathaniel out of their room, and how he dismembered Joshua's Lego army, or deconstructed one of the Lego spaceships that had taken Joshua hours to build. My response to Bonnie would always be,

"Well, what did you do about that?"

"I told Nathaniel to stop it!"

"And?"

"And then he went back and started terrorizing his sister all over again."

"And so what happened after that?"

"After that I took him to the living room and put in a video…"

"What?"

"What do you want me to do?"

"Oh, I don't know, how about applying a little tough love to the seat of knowledge?"

"I can't do that; he's the baby!"

So Nathaniel came to be dubbed 'The King.' That little goober had the run of the house. He had diplomatic immunity, and needed it often. Daddy, however, had the right to revoke his immunity wherever and whenever he thought it was in Nathaniel's long-term interests.

The weeks passed quickly. June ran into July, which was a busy month for me. I had to return to college to prepare for the next semester of college work. The 27th of July came and passed, and we thanked God for doing what seemed impossible. "With men this is impossible, but with God all things are possible"

Matt. 19:26. As of that day we were legally entitled to file with the court as "interested parties" in Nathaniel's custody hearing.

That summer was the last summer that I had with my motorcycle. For the last two years I had had the pleasure of owning the most awesome, most finely tuned machine on two wheels. Actually it was just a 500cc street bike. When we decided to hire a lawyer, I had to sell it to help pay for his retainer. I remember several weeks after I got rid of it when a close friend of mine came up to me and said,

"Hey, I just wanted to tell you that I think what you did was really cool."

"What are you talking about?"

"I heard that you sold your motorcycle to help pay for the lawyer. You know that there are men out there who wouldn't part with their stuff, even for something as important as this."

"Well, it wasn't a hard choice. My boy is more important than any old motorcycle."

"Well, just the same, you have my respect, bud!"

"Thanks, man."

I was glad to have a friend like Mike Fowler. He was a person who loved the Lord and who had prayed with me many a time as I went through this experience. Mike had expressed that he admired my self-sacrificial act, and I appreciated him for that, but I didn't have the heart to tell him that my motivations weren't totally pure. I did sell my bike to pay for Nathaniel's lawyer, but I was already planning out how I was going to use this to try and convince my wife to let me get a bigger and better one after Nathaniel's adoption went through.

August 27, 2002

From the 12th of June to about the beginning of August, we did not hear a word from anyone, not the Case Worker, not the Johnsons, not even our lawyer. Then one day Bonnie received a phone call and was informed that the Johnsons had re-filed their petition for custody and that the judge would be granting them a date. The preliminary date was the 27th of that month.

I have to admit, the first time that I found out about the new court date I began to experience those same familiar feelings all over again. The shortness of breath, the fear, the anxiety... I had to mentally 'slap' myself in order to stop fretting. I had no reason to worry anymore. God had given me the sign I was looking for; to be upset and nervous now would be ridiculous and would show a lack of faith. I made up my mind that the next time I walked into that courtroom I would do so knowing full well that I was not walking in there alone.

Now there were several things that had to be accomplished on that date. First, the court had to make a determination about the termination of both parents' rights. One parent was completed but the other was not. The judge decided to bundle the preliminary hearing for Johnsons' custody petition along with cleaning up the parental rights situation. Now that we were involved, the judge also had to consider that we wanted Nathaniel too. This promised to be a very interesting autumn. The 27th of August was also the first time that Bonnie and I met Nathaniel's aunt, Rose.

Up till this point I had dreaded going into that courtroom. Every time I entered that room my stomach would tighten up. But not so on that day. I remember when I walked into that courtroom on the 27th, I walked in with my head up, shoulders back, and a big grin from one ear to the next. I knew that there wasn't anything they could do. I had it on good authority that Nathaniel's case had already been decided. I determined in my mind that I was not going to allow myself to doubt as I did before.

The preliminary hearing went pretty smoothly. I don't remember very much of the hearing except that it ended quickly and that for the first time I felt that I didn't have to worry about what these people were going to do because I had my advocate involved and working on my behalf. And I'm not referring to my lawyer, Mr. Graham. I walked in there in confidence, and I left feeling that we would win in the end. It wasn't until later that night that I began to doubt all over again whether or not we were doing the right thing.

Social Services had scheduled the Johnsons' visit with Nathaniel for that afternoon. They wanted us to bring Nathaniel to a public park in town where we could meet with the Johnsons and their children, and they could interact with Nathaniel. The judge had hinted earlier that morning that maybe we should try and find a way to settle this without involving him. I didn't think that was possible, but I was grateful that we were allowed to stay there and keep an eye on Nathaniel.

Rose seemed like a very nice person. She was friendly to us and even referred to Bonnie and I as Nathaniel's mom and dad. We were able to talk about this situation, and we were able to get a lot of things out in the open. It was at this meeting that James quietly admitted to me that the missed flight was his doing. I believe that James wanted Nathaniel to stay with us but that he was going along because of his wife's wishes.

There was a part of our visit with the Johnsons that really caused me to doubt whether or not we were doing the right thing. During our conversation, Rose said that Nathaniel should be given to them because they were his 'real' family. She told us that she thought adoption was for children who did not have a home to go to. And since Nathaniel was wanted, he should not be allowed to live with anyone other than his real relatives. At one point she looked at both Bonnie and me and said, "You are not Nathaniel's real parents, you are not his family." She wasn't saying it in a hateful way, but the words cut deep nonetheless. She kept talking about how she loved Nathaniel (someone she had only seen once) and how he deserved to be with them. Bonnie and I responded to some of the things that she said, but we tried to keep the conversation polite. I had to suppress the desire to tell this woman off, and point out that if they had made attempts to be here on the 12th of June, this would not be happening right now. After approximately two or three hours the visit finally ended and Bonnie and I took Nathaniel and drove home. I tried to forget the things that she had said, but my mind kept replaying those words about Nathaniel needing to be with family, and how we were keeping him from them.

That night I really struggled with what we were doing. *"If this is the right thing, why do I feel like it's so wrong?"* Bonnie and I both were bothered by our visit with the Johnsons. We felt we were doing the right thing, but one question that kept popping up was how we were going to explain to Nathaniel how we fought to keep him from being returned to his genetic relatives. I really struggled with this. I don't really know why. It was almost as if Rose had cast a spell on me. I felt unsure, afraid. I began to wonder if I was keeping Nathaniel for the right reasons. Bonnie and I stayed up late talking about our fear that maybe we weren't doing right by Nathaniel. I remember at one point praying to God for guidance. I didn't understand how we could be so close to ending this thing and now feel as if we were doing the wrong thing. *"Maybe God wants us to voluntarily give up Nathaniel?"* I felt a feeling that I had not felt before. It was guilt! I actually considered calling the whole thing off and letting the Johnsons take Nathaniel. For the first time I began to doubt that Nathaniel would be better off with us.

I tried to come up with a reason to convince myself that Nathaniel was better off with us. But the more that I thought about it, the more I felt as if I was doing the wrong thing.

I hate indecision! I don't like to be around people who can never make up their minds and keep going back and forth. I hate that trait; especially when I do it. And now I felt anger, and guilt. I prayed some more…as I prayed I began to replay in my minds eye all the events that had brought my family and me to this point. I remembered what the intentions of the Johnsons' had been. I remembered that it was there lack of attendance on June 12th that placed Nathaniel, and us in this position. I also reminded myself that a family is not solely defined by sharing the same genetic markers, but by sharing a far stronger bond, love. There is a saying that "blood is thicker than water", I believe that "love is thicker than blood."

I had finally had enough! In that instant I made up my mind. I looked at Bonnie but I was really speaking to myself, "What in the world am I doing? Nathaniel belongs here! **We** are his family, we're all he knows. God wants Nathaniel to be here! We've been the ones taking care of him, feeding him, changing him, and staying up with him when he's sick. Nathaniel is here today because **they** failed to do their part!" —I could still hear her words, "You are not his real family!" ringing in my ears. These words caused me to be angry, and concerned that we were doing the right thing. But I decided to go forward and not second guess myself anymore.

Maybe what really bothered me was that she had said some things that hurt me and she didn't hold back, but I did. Maybe I was angry because she had gotten the last word in? —Well now, I couldn't have that! —I knew that the Johnsons were leaving in the morning, so I decided that I would find them and respond to the comments she had made that afternoon.

I had no idea where they stayed that night. I had heard James say that they had a hotel room in town but he didn't say which hotel. I had purposed in my mind to find them though, so early the next morning I left for town and went looking for them. There are approximately eight different hotels in town; so I just went to the first one I came across, an Econolodge, and drove into their parking lot. And sure enough, their van was there. "Thank you,

Lord!" I said aloud. I was worried that I would be too late to catch them because they were leaving for Tennessee that morning.

It was 6:30 a.m. I had the hotel clerk call them down. They both looked surprised, and disheveled. I think they thought I had come to tell them that they could take Nathaniel. Yeah right! —We had a long talk that morning. I had been afraid to tell the Johnsons what I really thought because I didn't want to cause a scene at the park, but this time I didn't hold anything back. I told them that Nathaniel was our son if for no other reason than because of the bond of love we have with each other. I also told them that they were responsible for what was happening now because of their failure to show up on the 12th of June... I also told them of my prayers, and my belief that God wanted Nathaniel to stay. They were Christians also, so I thought they would understand, but Rose's response was that she thought God wanted Nathaniel to go with them. In the end we decided to both go forward and let the judge decide Nathaniel's fate. We both agreed that we would let God decide and that decision would be manifested in the judge's ruling. I went to work that morning feeling at peace, and troubled. I still believed that God wanted Nathaniel to stay, but I wondered if God granted my petition because of my persistence, or because it was right for Nathaniel.

August was also interesting because of something else that occurred. Bonnie received a phone call from Social Services and was told that Hannah, our daughter, had a half-brother, Scottie, a three-month old baby who needed a home for a possible permanent placement. We had provided respite for Scottie a couple of times during the summer, but we were told that he would not be freed for adoption. When Bonnie called me, I said,

"NO WAY, NO WAY! Are you crazy? We already have four children!"

"But he's Hannah's brother; we can't just let him go anywhere."

"——(a long pause), (another long pause) Fine! We can try it. But I'm not running an orphanage here."

"I know that! What other choice do we have?" Of course, she was right. Hannah's going to have a lot of issues to deal with when she gets older, worrying about Scottie should not be one of them.

In time Scottie earned his nickname, Scottie-go-Pottie. Whenever it was time to change him, we not only had to change his diaper but his onesie, his socks, and his shirt. This happened once a day, everyday. Bonnie was in heaven, and hell. As Scottie got older and began to walk, he and Nathaniel became double the fun, and double the trouble. They were beautiful, healthy, demanding, and very loud. The exploits of Butch and Sundance could be the subject of a separate book.

One of their favorite things to do was to remove all the videos off of the bookshelf in our living room and take all the children's books on the bottom shelf, and scatter them all over the floor. But that wasn't the best part. The best part was when Bonnie or I came out and caught them. The two of them would scatter in different directions as if they knew that what they did was wrong. Nathaniel was older so he could run faster, but Scottie—all he could do was waddle on his tippie-toes as fast as he could. He motored right along until he came to a corner. Since he couldn't turn quickly enough he would just fall down, turn his body in the direction he wanted to go, and then stand up and take off again. Somewhere in the Bible it states that children are a treasure from the Lord. It also states, "Happy is the man whose quiver is full of them." I had enough arrows in my quiver to outfit a small regiment.

A setback

The process of freeing Nathaniel for adoption required that the rights of Nathaniel's biological father be terminated. Social Services had been given the date of October 17th, 2002 for that hearing. I was present at that hearing even though I did not have a part in what was going on. I had my lawyer present there also. All we could do was just watch the proceedings. According to the law in New York, a parent's rights can be terminated if they do not have any contact with Social Services for six consecutive months. If a child is placed in the foster care system and the parent does not contact Social Services or the child for six months, then Child Protective Services can file for termination of rights due to "abandonment." This was what Social Services was attempting to do. The bio-dad was not present at the hearing, but the lawyer that the court appointed to represent him was. This hearing took place before Judge Lawless and all the same lawyers that had been involved in Nathaniel's custody hearing.

The situation was not as clear-cut as I had hoped. In order to prove abandonment, the law states that there has to be no contact whatsoever. As the hearing went on, I learned that the bio-dad had contacted Social Services on two occasions but he never followed through on anything that he said he was going to do. The Social Services lawyer was trying to prove to the judge that the bio-dad did not make any real attempt to work with his department. And I thought he did a pretty good job at it. However, the law states that no contact is required to determine that a child has been abandoned. So it was up to the judge to decide what constituted 'contact.' The hearing lasted several hours, and the judge told us that he would not rule that day, but would rule in the coming days and notify everyone in writing. I left feeling that the case had been made that Nathaniel had been abandoned by his biological father.

I expected that the judge would rule rather quickly on this issue. But in fact we did not hear from the judge for several weeks. This concerned me but I didn't let it bother me too much because I knew in my heart that Nathaniel was going to stay. So the days turned into weeks, and the weeks turned into a month. It was near the end of November when I received word that the judge had ruled on the issue of termination of the father's rights.

The judge had ruled that because there was some contact between the Case Worker and the bio-dad, the case had not been made legally for abandonment. Therefore he had no choice but to dismiss the request of Social Services to terminate the father's rights. I was speechless. I thought that we had this thing all but finished. In order for Bonnie and I to adopt Nathaniel, we had to clear this hurdle first. Just when I thought that things were running along quite smoothly we had this happen.

I thought I knew what God was up to. I believed that He had tipped his hand to me earlier this summer and that the rest was going to be smooth sailing. I knew now that this was not going to be the case.

"I don't think I can take anymore of this, Lord! If you don't stop this circus I think I'm going to have a heart attack!" That was my feeling. I was beginning to get physically ill all over again. That evening I had to do some soul searching. My hope had been that if the judge had terminated the bio-dad's rights, then maybe the Johnsons would have backed off, thinking that it was God's will for Nathaniel to stay. But now with this victory for their side, I knew that they would fight on, believing that God had given them a sign to go forward. It seemed to me that God was toying with our emotions, and with the Johnsons' emotions. It seemed to me that God was playing both sides against the middle. —Whose side was He on, anyway? Those were my initial feelings.

It took me some time, but eventually I came to my senses. I had gone into this ordeal believing that God would ultimately do what was in Nathaniel's best interests. I <u>knew</u> that the Lord's hand was controlling what was happening here, even if I didn't understand it. I remembered my conversation with God when I told Him that I would abide by whatever He allowed to happen. I truly didn't know what God had planned, but I decided once again that if God wanted Nathaniel to go to live with the Johnsons, then I would accept it. One question haunted me throughout this time. Did God allow Nathaniel to stay because it was in his best interests? Or did God allow Nathaniel to stay simply because I had bombarded heaven with my prayers? I loved my son, but I also wanted what was best for him. So after much soul searching and hand wringing, Bonnie and I, once again, decided to let God be God. He would decide what was the best place for our son. And we would accept it. Again, just as at Camp Cherokee, I felt a sense of peace come over me. I knew that whatever happened next, it would be because God had willed it to be that way.

Dec. 12, 2002

The months passed, from June to November. I had been busy working on a project for college so the time passed by rather quickly for me. I remember when I contemplated dropping out of college and the director of the Adult Degree Program spoke with me. She told me that college might be just what I needed because it would give me an outlet for my stress. I didn't think so at the time, but as it turned out she was right. Being involved in my studies helped me to pass the time. This allowed me to not think about what was going on until we were close to the court dates.

At the end of November we received word from the court that the judge had decided to move forward with the custody hearing for Nathaniel. Judge Lawless had informed all involved that December 12th was the date for the custody trial. I didn't understand how he could do this. It was my understanding that the father's rights had to be terminated first. If the father's rights were not terminated we would be at a terrible disadvantage in court because his wishes would be considered at the trial. The bio-dad had made it very clear in his letters to the judge and through his lawyer, he wanted Nathaniel to be given to his sister.

Upon hearing about this new court date I went straight to my lawyer, Keith Graham, to find out what this meant for our case. As I anxiously sat in my chair, he calmly explained to me what would happen on the 12th and what part we would play.

"One of two things is going to happen." He said. "If the judge decides to give Nathaniel to the Johnsons, then the father's rights would be a non-issue, because the father has already let the judge know that he wants Nathaniel to go with them. If we are given custody of Nathaniel then I'll ask the judge to automatically rule that the bio-dad's consent is not needed for an adoption. My argument will be that although he has not technically abandoned Nathaniel, he has not shown any interest in the proceedings whatsoever to this point. I've done some research into this and found that other judges have done that."

"What do you think our chances are?" I asked.

"I can't say. I didn't expect the judge to dismiss the petition of Social Services to terminate ————————'s rights, but he did. Nothing has gone the way that I've expected it to. It's gonna come down to who the judge feels would take better care of Nathaniel. It's hard to know what this judge is thinking."

I remember looking at him just then... He didn't seem very optimistic. He believed that we had a strong case but he didn't seem too confident in our chances. I remembered just then all of the signs that Bonnie and I had experienced in the last few months. I wanted to share with him the confidence that I had, and also the reasons why. But I was afraid the he wouldn't understand. The truth is that part of me was embarrassed to tell him that God wanted Nathaniel to stay. I was too chicken to tell him that God had arranged this whole thing. I was afraid that I would say something and he would think that I was some kind of a wacko fruitcake. I was ashamed of myself because I couldn't seem to explain to him the reason for the hope that I had in me. How can I call myself a Christian, yet be afraid to share with others about the wonderful experiences that my God had brought me through?

The days leading up to the 12th of December flew by. I thought about the date, December 12th; exactly six months from the day that I thought I was going to lose Nathaniel. I had asked God to postpone the custody hearing until we could get legally involved and God had answered my prayer by granting me exactly six months.

I spent the days leading to the 12th mulling over a lot of issues, and questions:

Did God want Nathaniel to stay because of my persistence, or because it was the best thing for him?

Was Rose Johnson right when she said that Nathaniel needed to be with his biological family?

Were we denying Nathaniel his heritage by insisting that he stay with us?

Was she right when she said that Bonnie and I weren't his real parents?

Is a genetic relation more important than a bond of love?

Would God work things out so that the Johnsons would not be able to show up for this trial in the same way that they missed the first one?

The custody hearing had become a custody trial because there were two parties involved now. At this trial there would be witnesses called and evidence presented. This was going to be bloody. I suddenly realized that I hadn't spoken with any of the lawyers about what they thought was best for Nathaniel. At the trial there would be five lawyers present: the law guardian for Nathaniel, the lawyer for Social Services, my lawyer, the Johnsons' lawyer, and the bio-dad's lawyer. I didn't know if the lawyer for Nathaniel and the lawyer for Social Services were on my side, or the Johnsons' side. A part of me had been afraid to ask them. —I resolved not to allow myself to worry.

On the morning of the 12th, Bonnie and I delivered the kids to Grandma's house and drove into town for the trial. I don't remember anything in particular about that morning except for our usual family morning prayer. I thanked God for Nathaniel, and for the many miracles He had done, and for the miracle He was yet to do. I was all done crying, and pleading, and worrying about what was going to happen. I was ready to get this thing over with, once and for all. The children knew what that day was, but just as before, I told them that I believed that God would let Nathaniel stay, and that they shouldn't worry about it.

Our lawyer, Mr. Graham, had told us that his plan was to call each of us up to the stand so that we could tell the judge why we wanted to keep Nathaniel and give any evidence that we felt would be relevant to the judge in making his decision. Bonnie and I had prepared for this in much the same way as we did for the first hearing. We studied our notes and tried to commit every detail to memory.

I couldn't wait to finally be able to get on the stand. *"Just let that judge ask me why I want to keep Nathaniel,"* I thought. I had rehearsed over and over again my dissertation on why Nathaniel should be allowed to stay with us, and I couldn't wait to get on that stand.

The hallway leading to the courtrooms was packed that day, as it usually was. Bonnie and I looked around for any sign of the Johnsons, hoping that they weren't there. But to our dismay they were. We greeted them and even made some small talk before we went into the judge's courtroom. I didn't have anything against that family; I just wanted them to leave my family alone. I also expected to see Nathaniel's bio-dad there, but he did not show up, although his court-appointed lawyer did.

When the time finally came, all of the lawyers and our two families filed into that courtroom, which now looked too small to accommodate all of us. I brought some paper with me to take notes of the events of that day, for Nathaniel to look back on. I began by taking attendance:

Social Services Lawyer	Jack Day
Senior Case Worker	Angela Dow
Law Guardian	David Packer
Bio-dad's Lawyer	Gabe Willard
Johnsons' Lawyer	John Kupchak
Our Lawyer	Keith Graham
The Johnsons and the Crespos	

After the introductions the Judge got right down to business. First, the judge wanted to hear the opening statements of the lawyers. I guess he wanted to know where everyone stood before we got started. I was a little curious too. I had not spoken to any of the lawyers involved, so I did not know what to expect.

The first lawyer to speak was Nathaniel's law guardian. He stood up and composedly said,

"Your honor, Nathaniel has been living with the Crespo family since he was three months old. I believe that he has done very well, both emotionally and physically since he has been in their home. I understand that the Johnsons are seeking custody but I believe that it would serve no good purpose to remove him from the home where he is currently residing. I do not believe that it is in Nathaniel's best interests to be removed from the Crespos' home."

I was so happy I could hardly contain myself.

The next lawyer up was the one representing the department of Social Services. I knew that these two were the most important ones in terms of how much sway they had with the judge due to their supposed impartiality, so I listened intently. Remarkably, he echoed the sentiments of the law guardian.

"Your honor, I agree with Mr. Packer on this. I don't believe that it would be in little Nathaniel's best interests to be removed from the home of the Crespos."

He believed that Nathaniel should be allowed to stay where he was! This was better than I had hoped for. I really hadn't known what to expect, but this was great! I silently shot up a prayer to heaven, thanking God for his blessings.

I already knew where the others lawyers stood. Our lawyer was on our side. The lawyer for the Johnsons and the lawyer for the bio-dad wanted Nathaniel to be given to the Johnson family. So it was 3 to 2 in our favor. I knew that ultimately the judge would make the final decision.

The trial lasted all day. The first witnesses on the stand were the Johnsons: first James, and then Rose. I was shocked at the intensity with which the lawyers ripped into James. We had shared with all of them by now what we believed to be their intentions regarding Nathaniel, and the Social Services lawyer brought it all out. I was grateful that someone seemed to finally believe us. I was a little upset, however, at the response by James to some of the questions posed to him. There were things that he had told me earlier that he denied on the stand. I know that it didn't make sense for him to say something that would hurt himself, but as a Christian I still expected him to be honest. I would have been. One thing that was strange, which one of the lawyers brought up, was the question of whether or not they had made plans to visit Nathaniel today. They had two weeks notice of this trial, yet they had never called Social Services to schedule a visit for today, and this wasn't the first time that had happened. They hadn't even called the Case Worker to try to figure out what would be the best way to transition Nathaniel, although the lawyer never asked him about that. James had no response to the lawyer's observation. In a way I felt bad for him. I think he could have given a reasonable explanation if he wasn't so nervous. I'm glad he didn't though.

Something happened during the time that James was on the stand. After about an hour and a half, the judge called a recess so that we could all take lunch. I don't know for sure, but I believe that during this recess the judge instructed the lawyers to stop attacking Mr. Johnson. Our lawyer came up to us afterwards and told us that he was going to change his strategy. Instead of focusing on the Johnsons' weak points, he was going to focus on our strengths. I didn't understand why the change, but I heard him mutter something to the effect that he didn't understand why the judge had taken such a liking to the Johnsons.

After the recess the trial resumed. I had made a mental note of the questions that James was asked because I expected that they would ask me the same ones as well. When Rose Johnson took the stand, the lawyers asked her a series of questions. But it was now a kinder and gentler lawyer pool. These questions were more about their home life and their own children. The lawyers were trying to determine what kind of situation Nathaniel would be going to. At one point she was asked how they disciplined their children. The lawyer asked if she spanked her children. It was apparent that she was not sure how to answer that question because of how it might make them look. I knew that with as many children as they had (5), discipline had to include more than just a 'timeout'. Bonnie and I were sitting in the back when she leaned over and whispered, "If they ask me that question, I'm only going to answer for me." In other words, if they asked me that question I was going to be on my own. *"Please Lord, don't let them ask me that question!"*

After Rose, Bonnie took the stand. And again, they asked a series of questions, much the same as they had asked Rose. They did not ask about discipline in our house, however. The questions dealt with our home, our finances, etc.... Near the end of the questioning the judge asked my wife to tell him why Nathaniel should stay in our home. He had not asked that question of Rose. He had however, asked her husband James that question. James' response was that he wanted to take Nathaniel and raise him up as part of their family so that Nathaniel could know his real family and be a part of it.

When the judge asked Bonnie that question, I saw tears well up in her eyes. I thought that she was going to lose it, but she held those tears in her eyes so you could just see a glimmer of wetness around her eyeballs.

She said, "We love Nathaniel; he's a part of our family. When Miguel leaves for work Nathaniel is the last one waving at the window and the first one there waiting for him when he pulls into the driveway...(she was getting close to crying now). We love him, and he loves us. We've taken care of him, bathed him, stayed up with him when he's been sick..." As I remember, the judge didn't really let her finish. He just looked at her and said, "OK, thank you, Mrs. Crespo." I have to say that I was so proud of my wife that day. She had been nervous about being on the stand, but I thought she did an excellent job.

I thought that I would finally get my moment before the judge. I so badly wanted to have the attention of all the parties involved so I could tell them exactly what I thought. But it was not meant to be. During the recess my lawyer told me that I would more than likely not take the stand. He just wanted Bonnie, and the psychologist. We had a psychologist as a witness who told the judge about the negative effects that a child can experience if he or she is taken from a home and a family that he or she has bonded with. She believed, after meeting with Nathaniel, that it would be in his best interests to be allowed to stay where he was. There was very little in the form of cross-examination by the other lawyers. The psychologist was the last witness.

By the time the lawyers were all done asking the psychologist questions, the day was almost over. The judge, however, assured everyone that they would receive his verdict that day. He knew that the Johnsons had come a long way, and he did not want to draw this out any longer. I think that he was ready to finally end this thing as well. After the last witness, the judge asked the lawyers to each present a closing statement. This was to see if either of the two lawyers, the law guardian and the Social Services lawyer, had been swayed by what they heard. Thankfully, they hadn't.

Each of the lawyers received a chance to make a statement. Since the judge was the jury, the lawyers addressed him directly. The first lawyer allowed to address the judge was the bio-dad's lawyer.

He stood up and said, "Your honor, my clients' position has been the same throughout this whole ordeal. He has expressed to me that his wishes are for Nathaniel to be handed over to the Johnson family. I, uh, well, my client does not want his son to be adopted by another family. He feels that it would be better for Nathaniel to be raised by a blood relative."

He didn't sound too convincing to me. I noticed that his body language did not seem to go along with the words that were coming out of his mouth. It seemed to me that he was doing his job in representing his client, but that his heart wasn't in it. It seemed to pain him to say that Nathaniel should be removed from our home. At least it looked that way to me.

Jack Day, the Social Services lawyer, stood up when it was his turn and said to the judge, "Your honor I believe that there are two good options for Nathaniel." I was surprised to hear him say that. "Either situation would be good for Nathaniel. But as you heard the psychologist say; to remove Nathaniel from the family that he has bonded with can have devastating consequences to his psyche. I just don't see any good reason to remove Nathaniel from the situation that he is currently in. It's obvious that the Crespos love Nathaniel. And he has also done very well, developmentally speaking. It is the opinion of the department that he should be allowed to stay with the Crespos."

I was glad to hear that he wasn't swayed by the testimony of the Johnsons'.

The next lawyer to close was the Johnsons' lawyer. I was not impressed with the way that he questioned the different witnesses, but I was impressed with the argument that he closed with.

He said, "Your honor, Nathaniel deserves to be with his family. The Johnsons have offered to take him in and raise him. It is the goal of Child Protective Services to place a child with relatives whenever possible. Nathaniel's relatives have stepped forward. If you choose not to give Nathaniel to the Johnsons, Nathaniel will still be the responsibility of the Department of Social Services. In other words, Nathaniel's future will still be in limbo. Your honor, you have the power to end this nightmare for little Nathaniel. By giving him to my clients you can close this case for the department and allow Nathaniel to move on with the rest of his life. You can close this chapter in Nathaniel's life."

He referred to Nathaniel as being a child in limbo, and he said that the judge had the power to bring this limbo to an end. He was right to a certain extent. If we got the chance to adopt Nathaniel it would not take place for at least another six months. Which means that Nathaniel would technically still be in the foster care system. From a financial standpoint it made sense to release him now so that the court could move on to other issues.

Our lawyer, Keith Graham, was next. I have to say that if the Johnsons' lawyer had hit a homerun in his closing statement, then Graham hit a grand slam!

"Your honor, Nathaniel has been a part of the Crespo family since he was three months old. He has become a part of their family and they have become a part of his. They are the only family that Nathaniel knows. I would remind the judge about the testimony of the psychologist. She said that the damage that Nathaniel would experience by being removed from the Crespo home could stay with him forever."

As he was speaking to the judge, I was touched with how he addressed Judge Lawless. It was almost as if he were pleading for his own son. I noticed that as he spoke to the judge, his voice broke up. It seemed to me he was empathizing with us and relating that to the judge. Finally, he said something that I had wanted to say from the very beginning: "Your honor, the Johnsons' talk about how much they love Nathaniel. But in fact, they are nothing but strangers to him. Rose Johnson has only seen Nathaniel once! The only family that Nathaniel knows is Mr. and Mrs. Crespo." I wanted to jump up and shout "Amen!!" but I didn't.

The last lawyer to close was Nathaniel's law guardian, David Packer. Throughout the trial I had tried to determine what he might have been thinking about what was said on the stand. —He would make a great poker player. I couldn't get anything from watching his facial expressions. When it was his turn, he stood up from where he was sitting and said, "Judge, I don't put a lot of stock in emotion or in the diagnosis of the psychologist. The truth is that Nathaniel might be traumatized from removal, but he also might not. So that doesn't mean a whole lot to me. I believe that the Johnsons and the Crespos are equal in many ways. I believe that Nathaniel would be happy in either home. But I also believe that because Nathaniel has already bonded with the Crespos, he should be allowed to remain in their home." Again, I quietly thanked God for this little miracle.

Finally we were at the end. Everyone had gotten a chance to address the judge. All the witnesses, all the evidence, and all the arguments had been made. It was finally up to the judge to weigh the evidence and make his ruling. I watched as the judge suddenly got up and said, "Don't anyone go anywhere. I'll be right back." And with that he got up and left the bench, entering a room off to his right. As he closed the door, I saw him let out a big sigh. I could tell that this was not an easy decision for him. This made me a little uneasy, but at this point there was nothing I could do except wait, and pray.

The judge was gone for about one minute. In that time Bonnie and I held hands and silently prayed within ourselves, while the lawyers moved around in their seats and shuffled through the papers that they had tucked away in their open briefcases. Finally the judge returned and sat back down in his seat. At that moment time seemed to stop for me. *"This is it!"* I thought to myself, *"This is it, this is it, this is it! I could really lose Nathaniel! That judge can do whatever he wants. He can rule that Nathaniel is better off with them, and I may never see him again. What am I going to do? ——Where is your faith, man? God has brought you this far. Your whole adult life you've been talking about how you believe you can trust God. Do it now! —Whatever happens, I will trust in God!"*

"This is a very difficult decision," the judge began. "Usually in my line of work I have to choose between a bad choice or a not-so-bad choice, for a child. This is one of those times when there are two good choices for a child. I wish that I could give each family a child, but I can't."

My mind raced, *"What's he talking about? There is only one real choice for Nathaniel, and that's to stay with us. I'm gonna lose him, I'm gonna lose him...."*

The judge looked down and shook his head. "This is a tough decision: the decision is the Johnsons,"

Time stood still once again, *"Oh no! Oh no!"* I felt something like a weight fall, from my chest all the way down to my feet.

"It has to be my heart!" I thought.

"So this is what it's like to lose someone you love? (I paused in my thoughts for a moment) What am I going to do now?" All I remember was looking straight ahead of me at the judge's bench. I thought about the County Court insignia that I had seen engraved somewhere on this floor of the building.

"Someone had put an awful lot of effort into that intricate pattern. Those block letters looked easy to break off. I wonder if they glued them in or if they're nailed in?" I think I was in shock.

"Thank you Lord! Thank you for giving me Nathaniel, for allowing him to be a part of our life. Thank you..."

"or the Crespos." the judge finished.

"He paused, he paused, thank God he paused! —What's he trying to do? Give me a heart attack? I could kill him! —This means that we still have a chance!"

I admit that I didn't hear very much of what he said after that. The judge seemed visibly shaken. I'm not exactly sure why, but after some words that I really wasn't listening to, I heard him say, "I'm sorry (pause) Mr. and Mrs. Johnson, but I can't take Nathaniel out of the Crespos' home. If he were a couple of months old that would be a different story. But Nathaniel has grown up in that home and has developed a bond with that family." And then he said the words that I had been dying to have someone say to the Johnsons. "Bonnie and Miguel Crespo are Nathaniel's real parents..." I almost jumped out of my seat.

"…It is therefore my ruling to deny the custody petition of the Johnson family and to allow Nathaniel to remain in the home, and custody, of the Crespo family."

Bonnie and I both shot up prayers to heaven, thanking our God for finishing what we believed He had started. We thanked Him for the miracle that was one and half years in the making. After the judge stepped out of the courtroom, I got up, went straight to James and gave him a hug. James gave me a firm embrace and shoved his phone number into my hand. We didn't say much to each other, but there was an unspoken understanding. He knew that this was where Nathaniel belonged. Rose, on the other hand, didn't take it so well. She refused to hug my wife or say anything to me. I knew that that would take some time. Bonnie and I spent the next few minutes making the rounds, shaking the hands of the lawyers who had been pulling for us. I was so happy that I even considered shaking the hand of the lawyers who had opposed us. After several minutes I collected my wife, and the both of us floated down the hallway to the elevator, and back home to our "Brady Bunch-like" family that now numbered FIVE.

May 14, 2003

It was a beautiful spring day. We were back in court before Judge Lawless. This time the whole Crespo clan was there. My friend Mike was there also. The Case Worker, Angie Dow, was there; Jack Day and Keith Graham as well. It had been five months since that fateful day in December. Finally the day had come. All faces wore smiles, some wore tears. For the first time since I had been in his court, Judge Lawless looked directly at me and smiled. As he went through the formalities I noticed that the smile had become contagious. Everyone had one on. Even the Case Worker, whom I had not been kindly disposed to. The appearance before the judge was simple. Judge Lawless stated that the hearing today was to finalize the adoption of Nathaniel. Part of the ceremony calls for the judge to ask the lawyer representing Social Services if they have any objections to the adoption. When Judge Lawless asked Jack Day that question, he turned to us and said,

"Your honor, we think very highly of the Crespos and do not see any reason why this adoption should not go forward."

"Very well," he said.

I don't remember all that the judge said because of the excitement, but I do remember that he put his signature to the document that testified to the whole world that Nathaniel was my son! His name from that day on would be Nathaniel Thomas Crespo.

I learned a lot that day. I noticed how happy everyone was. I expected that my family would be happy, but I didn't expect the genuine joy that shone on the faces of the judge and the lawyers, and even on the Case Worker. I didn't understand it until afterwards. All day long these people deal with broken homes, and broken people. Their whole day is filled with cases where they are exposed to situations that just break your heart. Children abused, abandoned, and in need of a better life. Unfortunately, there are not enough happy endings. To all those involved, this was a happy ending. They were relishing this moment almost as much as I was because for them, good moments were few and far in-between. I remember at one point hearing the Social Services lawyer say to me that people like Bonnie and me are what make his job worth doing. I gained a new appreciation for what case workers and these lawyers go through.

I also learned a lot about myself. I learned a lot about my God, and my faith. Faith to me means to believe that something is going to come to pass based on what is found in the Bible, not on what I see with my eyes. I also learned that I can trust my God to work things out according to His will. It is still true that it's easy to trust and obey God when things are going your way. But the real test comes when we are willing to follow God when things aren't going our way. The Bible says, "Seek ye first the kingdom of God…and all these things will be added unto you" Matt. 6:33.

I learned that I'm weak when it comes to having faith. I find that it's easy for me to praise God when times are good. But there have been times when things haven't gone well, and I've doubted that God cared about me. There have been times when I've wondered if everything that has happened in my life has just been coincidence. There have been times when I've wondered whether or not God really exists. I hate that part of myself. I know now that God is truly concerned about the issues in my life. He loves me! I can hardly believe it. What an awesome feeling it is to know that the Creator of the Universe cares about the circumstances in my life! And He doesn't just care about mine alone. He cares about yours too.

I never want to forget what God did for me throughout this time. As I look back, I realize that throughout that time my prayer life was never better. My talks with God were more serious, more complete, less distracted. My Bible study time was more productive. I learned more because I personalized the promises I found in its pages. I claimed the promises of Scripture as at no other time in my life. Trials are God's method of drawing us closer to Him and making us more like the people He would have us to be. Don't ever despair in trial; God promises us that He will never leave us comfortless (John 14:18).

I also learned that God doesn't need my help to do anything. I was bummed out because I didn't get a chance to testify and speak to the judge, but looking back, I think that God worked it out that way so that I would know that this victory was all His. I had nothing to do with it. I need to learn to trust in the power and providence of God more than in my own abilities.

Epilogue

As of the writing of this book, Scottie has officially become a Crespo. I'm going to have to cut out another section of the concrete slab so that we can add another print to it. When I was a young lad eyeing that skinny little girl who was to someday become my wife, I never in a million years guessed that we would end up with so many children. When we were told of Scottie's adoption date, I told Bonnie:

"After Scottie, that's it! We are done with the children thing!"

She looked at me and said, "You can't say that; you don't know what God has planned for us."

"I know that whatever it is, it doesn't involve more children!", "I hope!"

Appendix

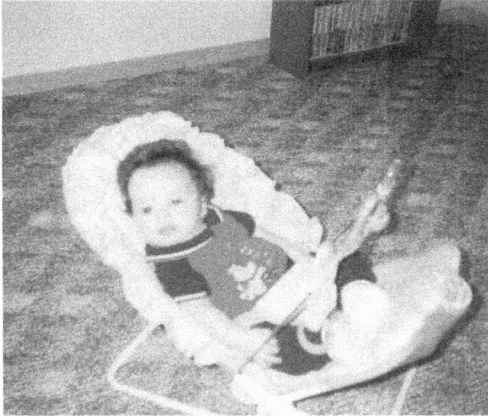

Nathaniel at 3 months.

Nathaniel officially becomes our foster child.

First famly photo of children.

Nathaniel at 10 months.

Crespo clan at home.

Nathaniel's adoption ceremony.

And they lived happily ever after.

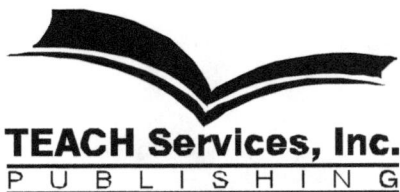

www.ingramcontent.com/pod-product-compliance
Lightning Source LLC
Chambersburg PA
CBHW070541080426
42453CB00029B/807